Brennan's   Royal St.

To Elizabeth & Hamish,
Bon Appetit &
Happy Cooking!

Thanks

Ruth Hughes

Published by Brennan's Inc.
417 Royal Street
New Orleans, Louisiana 70130-2191

Printed in the United States of America
Quebecor Printing Book Group

Library of Congress Catalog Card Number: 94-96530
ISBN 0-96398.19-0-0

Designed by Phillip Collier
Typography by Cox Electronic Publishing
Photography by David Richmond
Food Photography Assistant, Kurt Coste
Watercolor by Tommy Thompson, 1974

Second Edition

AND DINNER, TOO.

The original and most recent recipes from New Orleans' world-famous
Brennan's Restaurant and a tribute to its founder,
Owen Edward Brennan.

By Pip, Jimmy and Ted Brennan,
Proprietors

DESIGN BY PHILLIP COLLIER

PHOTOGRAPHY BY DAVID RICHMOND

DEDICATION

Owen Edward Brennan
1910 – 1955

May the road rise up to meet you.

May the wind be always at your back.

May the sun shine warm upon your face.

And rains fall soft upon your fields.

And until we meet again, may God

hold you in the hollow of His hand.

– an Irish Blessing

ACKNOWLEDGMENTS

Michael J. Roussel, Executive Chef

Lazone Randolph, Sous Chef

Harrison Duncan, Sous Chef

Kathy C. Abernathy, General Manager

Past and present staffs of Brennan's Restaurant

Ellen C. Brennan

Phillip Collier

Billie Cox

Terri Landry

David Richmond

Leon H. Rittenberg, Jr.

Bonnie Warren

Nancy Agnelly

Wayne E. Chambless

Kitty Foster Duncan

Roy Guste, Jr.

Barbara C. Heim

Eleanor C. Joseph

Emeril Lagasse

David Norris

Dawn Raymond

Al Shea

Katy Stewart

Richard White

Special thanks and love to Ellen for her dedicated hours of research, editing and supervision.

Ted

CONTENTS

INTRODUCTION

✥

$\mathscr{S}$ ince 1946, Brennan's Restaurant in New Orleans has been a culinary phenomenon. Through the years, Brennan's chefs have created some of the world's most famous and imaginative dishes which have given great pleasure to millions of discerning customers.

Chef Paul Blangé was the ingenious creator of many of Brennan's original signature dishes. Today, the influences of Chef Michael Roussel and Sous Chefs Lazone Randolph and Harrison Duncan maintain Brennan's as a restaurant rich in the traditions of its past while exemplary in the trends of the present.

At Brennan's inception, Owen Edward Brennan established the same standard of excellence nurtured today by his sons, Pip, Jimmy and Ted. As Owen received recognition from countless food critics, national publications and visitors around the world, Brennan's continues to receive culinary accolades. Among its many awards is the coveted Wine Spectator Grand Award for its outstanding wine cellar.

In the restaurant's most recent cookbook, Brennan's shares its gastronomic secrets in over 200 recipes, old and new, so that you may recreate these very dishes in your own kitchen. Each recipe has been home tested to ensure its accuracy. It is important to note that many of the breakfast, luncheon and dinner items are interchangeable.

Significantly, Brennan's new cookbook is much more than a collection of recipes. In a tribute to its founder, the late Owen Edward Brennan, the following pages include nostalgic memorabilia, unique illustrations of intrinsic value and a logical and truthful history of the restaurant.

Owen Edward Brennan was the culinary renaissance man of his time. He brought his newly founded restaurant to epicurean heights, locally and nationwide, in a very short period of time while charming his way into the hearts of all who knew him.

Owen Edward Brennan devoted his life to the restaurant that influenced the course of New Orleans gastronomy. In appreciation, Owen's sons dedicate this book to their father's memory.

Owen Edward Brennan, Brennan's founder and "The Happy Irishman of the French Quarter," in front of his historical Old Absinthe House and his world-famous restaurant.

THE HISTORY OF
BRENNAN'S RESTAURANT

❧

$\mathscr{O}$wen Edward Brennan, the founder of Brennan's Restaurant, was born April 5, 1910, in New Orleans' "Irish Channel" to Owen Patrick Brennan and his wife, Nellie. Over a span of the next twenty-three years, Owen's younger siblings were born in the following order: Adelaide, John, Ella, Richard (Dick) and Dorothy (Dottie).

Owen was already married when Dick and Dottie were born. Shortly after their births, Owen Edward Brennan, Jr. (Pip)was born to Owen and his wife, Maude. In time, Maude gave birth to two more sons, James (Jimmy) and Theodore (Ted) providing Owen with three male heirs.

A young Owen Edward Brennan, 1913.

Throughout his adult life, Owen Edward Brennan was driven by his devotion and an undaunting sense of responsibility to support not only his own wife and three sons but his parents and siblings as well. His father, Owen Patrick Brennan, was a New Orleans foundry laborer, which had made supporting Nellie and their six children very difficult; and so, his eldest son, Owen Edward Brennan set out to make his fortune.

Actor Robert Stack in the "Secret Room" in the Old Absinthe House.

Owen's undertakings and endeavors included buying an interest in a gas station as well as a drugstore and becoming the bookkeeper for a candy company. He worked as a liquor salesman and district manager for Schenley Company and, finally, as the temporary manager of the Court of Two Sisters Restaurant.

*I*n September 1943, Owen purchased the business of the Old Absinthe House on Bourbon Street. The Absinthe House had been built in 1798 and was known to be pirate Jean Lafitte's secret hangout. As its most recent proprietor, Owen staged lifelike mannequins of the notorious Lafitte and Andrew Jackson in what he called the "Secret Room" - the very room in which the pact was supposedly made in New Orleans' defense against the British at the Battle of New Orleans.

Owen became one of the city's best known hosts at his colorful Old Absinthe House, "the oldest saloon in America." Pianist Fats Pichon added to its charm with his talented renditions from Bach to boogie.

Actor Joseph Cotton and co-star Theresa Wright ("The Steal Trap") outside the Old Absinthe House.

Pianist Fats Pichon at the keyboard of the Old Absinthe House, Owen E. Brennan and guest look on.

Pianist Fats Pichon caresses keyboard regularly at famed old Absinthe House. His stylized singing parodies popular songs for patrons at Vieux Carre spot.

DIXIELAND RESOUNDS IN OLD CITY

Drummer Fred Kohlman is Mardi Gras favorite, was selected by television star Jack Webb to appear in film "Pete Kelly's Blues."

The historic Old Absinthe House.

The Chattanooga Times, June 1954

The Legend Will Grow
Bert Struby

NEW ORLEANS — So many stories have been told and retold so many times during the two centuries the famed Old Absinthe House has reposed leisurely on Bourbon Street here that some of them are becoming legends.

This story is not old enough to be a legend because, comparatively speaking, it happened almost yesterday. But someday it will be a legend and will join the other lore about the historic locale where it actually happened.

The hero and heroine in this story will not be named because they still live, perhaps in Georgia. But other visitors in years past who figure in other stories include Andrew Jackson, Gen. Robert E. Lee, Jenny Lind, William Howard Taft, John D. Rockefeller, Gen. John Pershing, Babe Ruth, and Franklin D. Roosevelt, to name a few.

STRUBY

For, you see, the Absinthe House outdates the Declaration of Independence by 24 years and a lot of things have happened beneath the hand-hewn cypress beams which support its ceiling.

More than a decade ago Owen Brennan, present owner of the famous tavern, suggested that visitors might attach their calling cards to the inside walls of the tourist attraction. The idea took and today literally thousands of cards and autographed slips of paper hang from the ceiling and walls.

Thereby also hangs this story.

It was late one evening a year or so after World War II that a young man entered, ordered himself a drink, casually walked over to a side of the room, disinterestedly began reading names on the cards.

❖ ❖ ❖

YOU COULDN'T find a particular card in days if you were looking for one, they are so numerous. And this former GI wasn't looking for any; just exercising idle curiosity to pass the time.

Suddenly he gave forth with a cry of surprise and delight.

Shouting excitedly for directions to a telephone, he dashed to the booth and placed a long distance call to Atlanta, Ga.

His party answered, he closed the door — and talked for a long, long time.

When he emerged, he could say only four words and he said them over and over:

"I've found my wife."

"I've found my wife."

"Don't you understand? I've found my wife!"

"That card over there. I've found my wife!"

❖ ❖ ❖

ULTIMATELY, WHEN he regained a semblance of composure, he pieced together the story about how he had been held prisoner during the war, his wife had been notified he was missing in action, and he had been released only at the end of hostilities.

Before he went overseas, they had lived in a small apartment in Cincinatti. Neither he nor his wife had any close relatives who would know their whereabouts. When he returned to Cincinatti to seek his wife, she had moved without leaving a forwarding address. No one knew where she had gone.

He had searched frantically, almost given up hope of finding her.

Then he read the card. It gave her name and business address. The telephone operator did the rest.

"I've gotta get the next plane to Atlanta," he exclaimed. "I've found my wife! She told me to come as quickly as I could!"

And off he went.

There's an adage about "Fools names and fools faces are often seen in public places."

But I wonder. Perhaps the Old Absinthe House is an exception.

The calling card walls and ceiling of the Old Absinthe House.

Owen created another dimension of ambience to the historical and musical atmosphere of the Old Absinthe House by inviting myriads of visitors to attach their business cards to its inside walls. Eventually, thousands of cards and autographed papers hung from its ceiling as well.

Owen hosts John Wayne "The Duke," Bruce Cabot and lady friend at the Old Absinthe House Bar.

Owen's customers could recapture the past with a Pirate's Dream, the specialty drink of the Old Absinthe House. He labeled it "the high brow of all low brow drinks." Owen perpetuated the popularity of the Absinthe Frappé, an original creation of the Absinthe House and a favorite of Presidents Franklin D. Roosevelt, Dwight D. Eisenhower and Admiral Earnest King.

*Y*et the adventuresome drinks and unique atmosphere of the Old Absinthe House were not Owen's essential keys to success. Owen Brennan didn't need frappés but only the flash of his smile and a warm welcome to his many customers. It was once written that Owen would hit his customers over the head with his personality - "a blow from which few tourists, writers, movie celebrities or presidents ever completely recovered." With this innate ability to win friends and customers while committing each and every one of their names to memory, it was no wonder that Owen would become a distinctively successful restaurateur.

"Since a restaurant with the unlikely name of Brennan's began serving some of the best French food in New Orleans, the mixing of nationalities is spreading across the country."

Chicago Daily News,
September 12, 1953

Original Brennan's menu.

Night lights shine from the Old Absinthe House and Vieux Carré. They face each other across narrow Bourbon Street

PHOTOS FOR COLLIER'S BY PHILIP GUARISCO AND WILFRED L. D'AQUIN

"Brennan's is certainly French and successful. Its specialties are as Gallic as they come, with Créole dishes – they're French once removed – it's extra special. This despite the fact that Brennan has breached many traditions that other French Quarter restaurateurs have always considered inviolate. That is, all the traditions except that of excellent food… But if Brennan flouted some traditions, he revived others. One notable fillip he brought back was the three-hour breakfast, a nineteenth-century custom supposedly unfitted to the modern tempo. There is one difference, however. Brennan grins owlishly as he points out, 'They used to charge from 40 to 60 cents. We get a lot more.' "

from "The Happy Irishman of the French Quarter" by Ken Gormin, *Collier's* Magazine February 18, 1950

"Night lights shine from the Old Absinthe House and Vieux Carré. They face each other across narrow Bourbon Street."

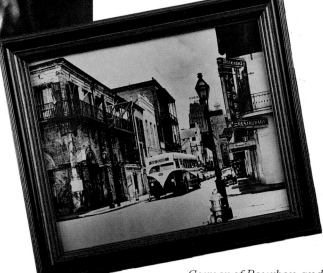

Corner of Bourbon and Bienville, 1952.

17

Owen's good friend, Count Arnaud, whose restaurant was a popular New Orleans dining spot, allegedly posed a challenge to Owen. Owen would relay complaints overheard at the Absinthe House to offending restaurant owners. To which Count Arnaud replied, "You're forever telling me about the complaints you hear. If you think you can do better, why don't you open a restaurant?"

At the same time Count Arnaud taunted that no Irishman could run a restaurant that was more than a hamburger joint. To which Owen responded, "All right you asked for it! I'll show you and everybody else that an Irishman can run the finest French restaurant in this town!"

In July 1946, Owen Edward Brennan leased the Vieux Carré Restaurant directly across the street from the Old Absinthe House. He named his new restaurant for himself, Owen Brennan's French & Creole Restaurant; and with time, it came to be more commonly known as Owen Brennan's Vieux Carré.

Owen employed his gray-haired father, Owen Patrick Brennan, as he feared injury would befall him in the shipyards. He then gave his father a small percentage of the business. Making his father a minority stockholder was Owen's way of providing and caring for his parents as well as his younger siblings.

*Telegram to
Owen E. Brennan
from Hank
Ketcham,
good friend and
creator of
"Dennis the
Menace."*

*"Brennan's Restaurant, in the
French Quarter of downtown
New Orleans at 241 Bourbon
Street, is nationally famous for
its fine French and Créole
cuisine. It is open from 9:00
a.m. until midnight on
weekdays. Breakfast, lunch,
dinner and late supper served
every day."*

*Atlanta Constitution,
1951*

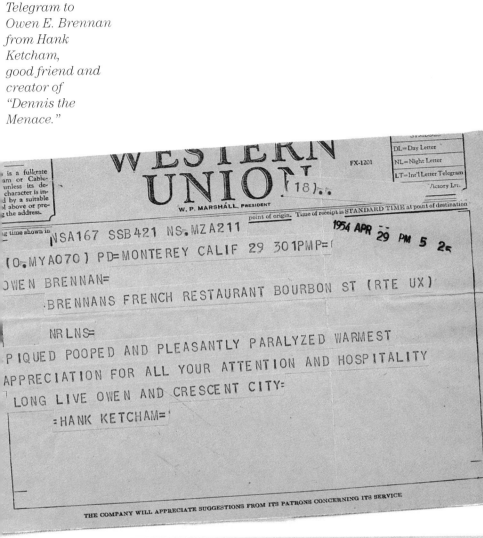

Owen E. Brennan featured in popular "Pogo" comic strip.

708 Tropical Blvd
Beverly Hills Calif —natch E.

HEDDA HOPPER'S HOLLYWOOD
702 GUARANTY BUILDING
HOLLYWOOD 28, CALIFORNIA

September 29, 1953

My dear Owen:

I don't know how you do it. You get no
sleep, but like that old man river, you just
keep rolling along.

After that wonderful breakfast, which I
drank with the greatest enjoyment, to be shown
around the French Quarter by you and Jill was the
greatest thrill I could imagine. I can just see
what you're going to do with the Absinthe House.
Gad, the history of that place!

I must say the plans for the 150th year
celebration of the Louisiana purchase are really
something. You don't stop at nothin'. I think
you're so right to bring the tourists down for
the summer. Just think of the thousands of shop
girls who long to see the city. They don't care
whether it's hot or cold -- just so it's New Orleans.

I loved the homey touch of the Stanley Marcuses
boarding the plane loaded down with French bread
from your restaurant. That Marcus is the smartest
man I know, next to you.

My best to you.

Always,

Hedda

Looking at Hollywood

BY HEDDA HOPPER

September 1953

I'M NOW ON A THREE
WEEK DIET because of a
three hour breakfast at Owen
Brennan's French restaurant.
But what a meal! Owen also has
a 90 year lease on the famous
Absinthe House. After the
breakfast, he and his sister took
a party of us on tour of the
French Quarter, which is loaded
with treasures, sights, and
historical documents. One item
was a three barreled gun,
outlawed many years ago
because it could kill from 150 to
200 birds at one firing.

20

The success or failure of this venture rested solely on the shoulders of Owen. Owen Edward Brennan had become the patriarch of the family. Everyone deferred to Owen. Many years his junior, Owen's siblings were either still youngsters in school or just starting out.

At Owen Brennan's Vieux Carré, Owen's father was found greeting the luncheon customers until a heart attack in the early 50's slowed him down. Eventually, Owen employed two of his younger sisters, Adelaide and Ella, as well as a younger brother, John. Adelaide became the bookkeeper and Ella the kitchen supervisor. John was employed by his brother for a brief time only.

Hollywood stars Robert Taylor and Barbara Stanwyck, (second and third from left), with other guests and Old Absinthe House proprietor, Owen E. Brennan (right).

Owen Edward Brennan and his Vieux Carré restaurant attained nationwide fame on an "Irish smile and a kiss of the Blarney Stone." Owen built his restaurant into a famous institution overnight, competing with New Orleans' oldest and best in French and Créole cuisine. Owen's research and knowledge of French food, fine wine and impeccable service made him a master. He was called the "wonder man" of the New Orleans restaurant industry. Owen's Irish stubbornness compelled him to work extremely long and hard hours to put Brennan's on the culinary map – locally and nationwide.

"Down on Bourbon St., we wandered quite accidentally into the man we were looking for – restaurateur Owen Brennan. He, too, was Southern hospitality personified."

Earl Wilson, June 1954

Walt Disney

Owen's ready wit, radiant smile and infectious laugh endeared him to locals, Hollywood celebrities and tourists alike. He was so very kind to so many people and was genuinely loved in return. As the famous novelist and syndicated columnist Robert Ruark once wrote about his good friend, "If he had a fault, it was his generosity." Owen was full of energy and possessed an incredible imagination; and all was reflected in Brennan's success.

Owen was known in Hollywood movie circles and entertained some of the brightest stars in his French Quarter restaurant – Vivien Leigh, John Wayne, Robert Mitchum, Barbara Stanwyck, Robert Taylor, Gary Cooper, Jane Russell and Tennessee Williams, to name a few. For national magazine writers and syndicated columnists, such as Earl Wilson, Walter Winchell, Hedda Hopper, Dorothy Kilgallen, Robert Ruark and Lucius Beebe, Brennan's was oftentimes their first stop on assignments to cover New Orleans. As a result, many stories were written of Owen's life and success in the restaurant business in national publications, such as *Newsweek, Collier's, Holiday, Life* and *Gourmet* magazines.

Owen E. Brennan toasts actor Walter Pidgeon and friend.

The advancement of the New Orleans community was high on Owen's list of priorities. He was especially devoted to the promotion of the New Orleans tourist trade and was labeled a "one man Chamber of Commerce." Appointed by Mayor Chep Morrison, Owen was the founding chairman of the first New Orleans Tourist Commission. He was a driving force as a member of the New Orleans Crime Commission and the city's Chamber of Commerce. As a promoter of the New Orleans tourism industry, Owen arranged a special Mardi Gras ball for visitors during the Carnival season.

Owen E. Brennan with celebrities Peter Lind Hayes and Mary Healy.

ELIA KAZAN

November 30, 1949

Dear Owen,

Just a note to thank you for the favors and the hospitality you showed me when I was in New Orleans. I mean, especially, about the house. That was a great help, and somehow or other I know we can get the whole bunch in there and they are all looking forward to coming to New Orleans. You will see them all first thing as I will bring them right in to the Vieux Carre and watch their faces as they eat those delicacies you dish out there.

Meantime, keep the take bigger than the nut and I will be seeing you.

Yours,
Gadg —

Mr. Owen Brennan
Vieux Carre Restaurant
Bourbon Street
New Orleans, La.

Left to right: Movie director Elia Kazan, Owen E. Brennan, actress Vivien Leigh and cinematographer Harry Stradling.

Maude and Owen Brennan

*Maude and Owen with
their three sons,
Ted, Jimmy and Pip.*

24

As a restaurateur, Owen Edward Brennan was a genius in a business for which he had no formal education. His creative ability was Brennan's crowning glory. After the publication of Frances Parkinson Keyes' *Dinner at Antoine's,* a new experience was conceived. Owen was convinced that if the concept "Dinner at Antoine's" could so successfully captivate a gastronomic audience, then why not "Breakfast at Brennan's?" And so Owen became the first in his time to promote this epicurean experience anywhere.

Owen at home with his family.

$\mathscr{B}$rennan's, as Owen ultimately wanted his restaurant to be called, became such a lucrative venture that when the time came to renew the lease on the Bourbon Street building, the landlord demanded fifty percent of the business. Unwilling to meet these demands, Owen searched for a new location for his restaurant and found its present location on Royal Street.

Maude and Owen Brennan

Owen was under a tremendous amount of stress as a result of his landlord's demands and his decision to move to Royal Street. At that time Royal Street was not the busy thoroughfare it is today. In fact, the Royal Orleans Hotel was not even in existence.

In 1954, Owen leased the building and began renovating and redecorating the Patio Royal at 417 Royal Street to convert it into the new Brennan's Restaurant. On November 1, 1955, Owen invited Brennan's initial customers to join him at his officially opened bar located in the building carriageway. The opening of the restaurant was scheduled for the spring of 1956, but the hand of fate dealt a devastating blow.

Anniversary Greetings
Love & Kisses, you lucky girl
Owen

25

Since the spring of 1950, Owen had been a member of La Confrérie des Chevaliers du Tastevin, an élite wine society whose original home was the Chateau du Clos de Vougeot, Côte d'Or since 1551. The objectives of the Tastevin were for its members to appreciate and promote the products of Burgundy and to maintain the region's festivities and customs.

Owen attended the fall dinner of its New Orleans chapter at Antoine's Restaurant on a Thursday evening in November 1955. That night no one enjoyed the exquisite wines, superb food and comradery of good friends more than Owen.

*T*he next morning, Maude was unable to wake her husband. At the age of forty-five, Owen Edward Brennan had died of a massive coronary in his sleep on a fateful Friday, November 4, 1955. Although shock and grief overwhelmed his family and the friends who loved him so dearly, Brennan's Restaurant still opened in its new Royal Street location on schedule.

At the time of Owen's passing, his sister, Ella, was thirty years old and was still the kitchen supervisor. Yet her strong will and leadership ability enabled her to assume the role of manager of Brennan's Restaurant. Owen's widow, Maude, had not been involved at Brennan's in a managerial capacity, and none of their three sons was old enough to affirm their positions as proprietors.

CHATEAU DU CLOS DE VOUGEOT
Home of the Confrérie

Owen at the fall dinner of La Confrérie des Chevaliers du Tastevin.

House Ap
has tentat
200,000,00
man's

FORE

Price 5 Cents

Friday, November 4, 1955

n Brennan Die

H

dely

Rest

City Will Miss Owen Brennan

A Truly 'Fabulous Orleanian'

Few men have ever been more a part of the life and traditions of our "Fabulous New Orleans" than Owen Brennan.

There was something wonderfully winning about this man from the Irish Channel and the happy-hearted way in which he built his restaurant into a famous institution, competing with the city's oldest and best in French and Creole cuisine.

Owen Brennan's cordial hostship will be sadly missed by the many thousands —here and everywhere—who knew him personally.

His death—at 45 and at the very height of his almost magical success—is also a serious loss for the community in general.

New Orleans' tourist business was part of Owen Brennan's trade. But it was more than that with him — it was his great enthusiasm. His interest in making this the great resort center of the South extended far beyond the walls of Brennan's restaurant and the Old Absinthe House.

In this cause, he gave generously of his own personality, energy and imagination. So much that he often kidded himself about being a "one-man Chamber of Commerce" for New Orleans.

For all this, as well as for the good will and good fellowship he offered all he met, New Orleans owes him much.

E. Brennan, fa
s sleep today.
nan was found de
morning by his w
years old. He li
est End Blvd.
nan was owner of
the House, Brenn
nd Creole Restau
n and Bienville.
o open a new p
Restaurant at
n.

NIGHT HE attende
nner of a gourmet
, the Confreti
du Tastevin. H
lained of illnes
20 pounds in th
eeks, friends said
rs include his w
Siener: thr

...AN DIES
...ME HERE

OWEN E. BRENNAN

Owner Of ...ITEM Restaurant

...rkets

r, cold.

...re

...own

...ateur

...leans restaurateur,

Farewell

Now and then I bid farewell in this column to some friend who has preceded me into whatever lies on the other side of the final curtain. I am reluctant to do so, be-

...RN AIRPLANE?

...many business-
...estion of learn-
...seen their own
...ft in their busi-
...panies reaping
...eed, flexibility
...rating a com-
...now the trend
...sportation is
...portions—over
...employed by

...learn to fly?'
...'Mu...

throughout the world will miss the radiant smile and infectious laugh of Owen Bre... with a sens...

controversial Echo Park Dam from their plan to develop power resources on the upper Colorado River.

Hermann Deutsch

would prepare tureen... delica...

Federal Government, making t... first under President Eisenhow... private "partnership" policy.

MILESTONES

Died. Owen E. Brennan, 45, New Orleans restaurateur, owner of Brennan's Vieux Carré restaurant (a three-hour breakfast at $9.45), and the Latin Quarter landmark across the street, the Old Absinthe House (founded c. 1805); of a heart attack; in New Orle...

Montmartre with a serenity t... the circumstances of his life. ... married buxom Lucie Pauwels... water in his wine, dropped an i... about him, appointed herself th... and sole... flag...

Owen Brennan

...better friends|ship was very fine. ... I suspect nobody has ever been quite so kind to so many ... as Owen Brennan, or ...ally loved in his ...a fault it

Robert Ruark

...down Bourbon St., they closed it up behind us, for Owen was a Pied Piper.

He never had the slightest interest in sleep, a fault I share, ... through him I got to know ...that I love, and

73...
191...
Ori...
aw...
Ar...
tic...

LEON URIS
Marine turned writer

"*An author of a best-seller might well be expected to talk about his latest book and the plot of a new one still in the typewriter.*

But at lunch at the Carlton House yesterday 31-year-old Leon Uris, the marine who wrote 'Battle Cry' spent most of the time chatting about his recent visit to New Orleans.

...we were on mutual grounds when the conversation swung around to New Orleans and one of that city's most famous gents – Owen Brennan ... After finishing with Greece, he doesn't have any particular locale in mind for his third book. It could well be about New Orleans and Owen Brennan."

Pittsburgh Press,
March 1955

30

May 16, 1955

Dear Owen:

The other nite Betty and I were fooling
around making Ramos Gin Fizzes.

I wish to report that I have discovered
a secret formula that makes mine far
superior to yours.

I will consider sharing this with you
for either half interest in your restaraunt
or Marcia Edgington.

Best wishes,

uris

P.S. It is done with voodoo.

also, my second novel is finished and
coming out this fall. If you play your
cards right I'll send you a copy.

At the time of their father's death, Pip was a graduating college senior, Jimmy a freshman in high school and Ted only seven years old. Immediately following his college graduation, Pip assumed a leadership role in the management of his late father's restaurant.

When Owen died, his photograph and the tragic news of his passing were front page headlines for New Orleans' *Times-Picayune* and *Item* newspapers. *Time* magazine included the calamitous report in "Milestones." Not only did nationally read Robert Ruark and New Orleans' own Herman Deutsch dedicate their columns to Owen Edward Brennan, but the editorial in the *Item* Sunday edition immediately following Owen's death was entitled "A Truly Fabulous Orleanian" in tribute to Owen.

In its new location on Royal Street, Brennan's prospered as it had on Bourbon Street. Owen's multitude of friends continued to patronize the restaurant he had founded even though their good friend was no longer there. Owen's ingenius concept of "Breakfast at Brennan's" and the dishes that were invented under his scrutiny, including Bananas Foster and Eggs Hussarde, combined with the expertise of his Dutch Chef Paul Blangé, had made Brennan's world-famous.

Owen's younger sister, Ella, inherited an enviable legacy in her position as Brennan's manager. Ella had learned most of what she knew about the restaurant business from her brother, Owen, whom

"…The greatest chamber of commerce man I know is an Irisher named Owen Brennan, a redheaded product of New Orleans' Irish Channel. Owen runs an ancient spot called the Old Absinthe House and a fine French restaurant called the Vieux Carré. Owen can't differentiate between 'oui' and 'non,' but he can shame a middle western Rotarian when it comes to plugging his town on a civil level. Both his establishments are about as wicked as a USO canteen, except the food and booze are better."

Robert Ruark,
New York Times,
June 2, 1950

31

she adored. Through the years Ella had observed not only Owen's technique in managing the daily operations but also his distinct style and finesse in dealing with the customers and news media. The mastery of public relations had been an exceptional expertise of Owen.

By maintaining Owen's many contacts and friends in the local and national news media, Ella was successful in her acquisition of publicity for Brennan's. She maintained Owen's friendships with numerous restaurateurs across the country and continued to promote Brennan's as a culinary mecca for celebrities.

*S*hortly after Owen's death, Brennan's needed additional working capital. Maude, Owen's widow, had already invested the money realized from her husband's life insurance policy in Brennan's, but these proceeds alone were not enough. Maude was advised by her late husband's good friend and financial advisor, Ralph Alexis, to offer her father-in-law, Owen Patrick Brennan, the opportunity to purchase additional Brennan's stock from her rather than allow non-relatives to become partners.

To provide the financial means, it was necessary that Maude's father-in-law borrow the money to purchase this stock. The cash proceeds from such a transaction would provide the business with the additional working capital. Maude heeded Ralph's advice and allowed her father-in-law to increase his percentage as a minority stockholder while maintaining control of Brennan's Restaurant for herself and Owen's three sons.

"Today, for a real treat in eating, come with me – won't you? – to Brennan's French and Créole Restaurant... Brennan's is owned, peculiarly enough, by a genial Irishman named Owen Brennan, who in a few years has established himself as one of New Orleans' best known hosts...I am inviting you to join me this morning for breakfast. This is not an ordinary breakfast, I hasten to assure you...to Owen Brennan it's a feast that could put the old Romans to shame... My bride had only one complaint, Owen's three-hour breakfast made us late for our four-hour luncheon at Antoine's!"

Kup's Column,
Chicago Sun-Times,
January 3, 1951

Breakfast at Brennan's

by Lucius Beebe

When the late Owen Brennan-founder of the fortunes of the House of Brennan, in the Rue Royale, in New Orleans - first undertook to promote and popularize breakfast in a public restaurant, his friends of whom there were many, shook their heads and confidently looked forward either to Brennan's bankruptcy or to a profound and immediate change of gastronomic heart. This was considered a mild view when his friends found that the menu would include a prescribed gin fizz, a claret, a champagne, fruit in brandy, and a dessert flamed in kirsch and strawberry liqueur in addition to such robust matters as broiled pompano, hot French bread, lamb chops with béarnaise sauce, exotically shirred eggs and *café diable*.

Even in New Orleans, a town where time means nothing and a great tradition of leisurely gastronomy obtains, this sort of thing was flying in the face of Battle Creek - where processed butcher's paper is widely packaged as breakfast food - not to mention the defying of an entire generation of Americans who have been conditioned, by means of one of the greatest national swindles of all time, to a breakfast of orange juice and Melba toast.

Brennan was goaded into prandial rashness when a lady novelist of some local fame had celebrated a rival restaurant in a novel called *Dinner at Antoine's*. Friends, growsing with Owen at this invidious partiality, came up with the alliterative of "Breakfast at Brennan's." The founding Brennan promptly ran up a collation that would have assured him of the patronage of Henry VIII and began advertising it as "an old New Orleans tradition dating from the great days of the Créoles," although the ink wasn't dry on the menus.

Brennan said that if nobody would eat his breakfasts he damn well would himself and promptly had his portrait painted opening a bottle of the best champagne. The portrait was prophetic, and it hangs today in a place of honor in a new and enlarged Brennan's much of whose fame, fortune, and felicitous repute derived from Owen's stewpot vision of what the morning of a civilized man should be devoted to. Under its benevolent regard, champagne corks mutter decorously of a Sunday morning and on weekdays, too, in an overture to a recurrent symphony of shrimp rémoulade and *café brulot* that is making Owen's heirs and assigns rich...

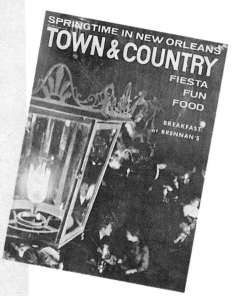

"Don't come to work without a smile on your face."

O.E.B.

NEW ORLEANS ITEM, Sun., Sept. 14, 1958

Robert Ruark

N. O. Revisited

I finally conquered my fear of returning to my favorite town, New Orleans, and hustled back for a quick evening. All the old ghosts have been properly laid. Most remain in their presence.

It has been 17 years since I first stood the Bourbon St. watch, but the scene remains the same.

A LOT of great people have died-Owen Brennan, Tom Caplinger, Bob Tallant, old Gasper, Jimmy Moran, three of the Weiss boys-but their ghostly presence is benevolent, and to each stands some sort of memorial.

It's as if they never really left, and I was almost surprised not be to met at the plane by the incomparable Brennan-the Irish poor boy who taught the local aristocrats what a fine French restaurant could be.

But for Brennan, who had dreams, and who signed for his dream the day before he died peacefully sleeping, as a young man, the dream is fulfilled.

He's been forced to move, because of lease difficulties, from his Vieux Carre, and he bought a long lease on a ramshackle building on Royal St. which is now, after a great deal of sweat and tears, the finest restaurant in the city, if not the country, if not the world.

There is not space to describe the elegance of a newly created Old World restaurant, from its tropical patio to its quietly lush rooms, its magnificent service and cuisine.

There is space to describe how the Clan Brennan-Owen's father, wife, brothers, sisters, sons, and the wives and husbands of all concerned, bent to the cause to make a dead man's dream of achievement come true.

* * *

BRENNAN WAS a rare, wonderful, generous and exceedingly intelligent man. He took New Orleans into his confidence, more or less, and eventually wound up, before he was 40, as the head man in the food and booze business, although he was fighting establishments like Antoine's, which had been legendary for more than 100 years.

The brash Mick from the Irish Channel was written and rewritten by national magazines-The Saturday Evening Post just recently ran a piece on a dead man's achievement-as the man who taught French to the French in terms of cooking and service and grace.

His new place with its lovely palm-studded, banana-fronded patio, could easily entertain a Madame Pompadour in one of its private dining rooms, and Escoffier would not sneer at what comes from the kitchen.

I live much abroad, and I have not seen elegance and grace done better in Paris or London. All of this transpires because a flock of redheads-Pop, Owen Junior, Adelaide, Ella and Dick-have worked like mad people to retrieve Owen Brennan's dream. Two thousand people now pay a daily homage to the effort, and the happy presence of Owen is still manifest.

* * *

He and I used to prowl the bistros of Bourbon St. until the dawn, and I prowled the street again on my visit with some of the heirs. The aura remained constant.

The people had died, and the people had left, but the street was the same, and I had a strange sort of feeling that Mr. B. was prowling along with one of his kids, one of his sisters, and a younger brother.

Papa Celestin is gone, but there are good loud horns on the street. Fats Pichon is still playing the Old Absinthe House, as he has done for a double decade or more.

And I was very proud to stumble into a place which advertised one Sharkey, the little man in the brown derby, whom I had not seen for at least eight years. I made a bet that when I walked in the door, Sharkey would quit blowing what he was blowing on his horn and break into a special piece.

I won my bet. He quit in the middle of "Muskrat Ramble," stopped his side men, and broke into a raucous version of my trademark tune: "Ugly Chile."

It was then I knew I was home, and having that late breakfast in Owen's memorial, I knew certainly and gladly that nobody had actually gone away except me, and now I was back again.

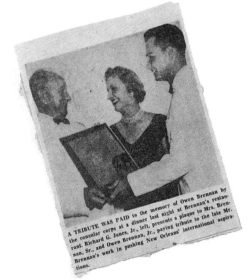

A TRIBUTE WAS PAID to the memory of Owen Brennan by the consular corps at a dinner last night at Brennan's restaurant. Richard G. Jones, Jr., left, presents a plaque to Mrs. Brennan, Sr., and Owen Brennan, Jr., paying tribute to the late Mr. Brennan's work in pushing New Orleans' International aspirations.

Owen Patrick Brennan and his wife, Nellie, died within a couple of years following the death of their son, Owen Edward Brennan. When Owen Patrick Brennan died, his minority interest in Brennan's Restaurant was divided among each of his own five surviving children and the late Owen Edward Brennan's three sons, Pip, Jimmy and Ted, further securing Maude and Owen's three sons as majority stockholders of Brennan's Restaurant. Until that time, Owen Patrick Brennan's children, Adelaide, John, Ella, Dick and Dottie, had not been stockholders in the restaurant.

As time passed, Ella sought to enlarge her legacy. In 1963, under Ella's management and direction, Brennan's Restaurant purchased the Friendship House Restaurant in Biloxi, Mississippi. At that time, Ella's expansion plans began.

𝒯he stock of each expansion restaurant – financed by Brennan's Restaurant and Owen's widow, Maude – was divided equally among the nine stockholders of Brennan's and not as the stock was divided in Brennan's itself. Thus, Ella and her siblings, who comprised five of the nine Brennan's stockholders, assumed control of the stock in each expansion restaurant while Maude and her three sons became the minority stockholders.

"…Of all the people who had gone, Alec missed Ben the worst. But he wouldn't go to New Orleans any more, on account of Owen Brennan's heart. He was leary of Houston, on account of Gran Adams' heart – hearts that had suddenly refused to work for no real reason known to anyone else but God…"

The Honey Badger
by Robert Ruark

Ella continued to expand the Brennan family operations. The opening of Brennan's Restaurant of Houston in 1967 was next. Jimmy, Owen and Maude's second son, moved to Houston to manage that operation. Jimmy had been formally trained in the restaurant business at École Hôtelière de la S.S.H. in Lausanne, Switzerland.

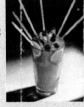

As one of four famous hosts, Owen E. Brennan endorses Rums of Puerto Rico.

Brennan's of Houston benefitted from Jimmy's knowledge of food, service and wine and was extremely successful under his management.

*B*rennan's of Dallas opened in 1969 with no Brennan family member in charge of its operations. A manager was hired by Ella and the pitfalls of expansion with absentee ownership became apparent.

In the spring of 1970, Ted, Owen and Maude's youngest son, moved from San Francisco, where he had been working since his college graduation, to take over the Dallas restaurant with high hopes and serious expectations of redeeming its reputation. By the time Ted arrived in Dallas as the restaurant's newest manager, Brennan's had been opened for fourteen months and was operating in the red with little hope of recovery. However, after much hard work, duress and his own Irish stubbornness, Ted was able to turn Brennan's of Dallas around, win back many of its initial customers, cultivate new ones and, finally, show a substantial profit.

In 1969, the Brennan family also purchased an established New Orleans restaurant, Commander's Palace, as well as a family-style restaurant in Metairie called Chez Francais. After the opening of Brennan's of Dallas, plans for a Brennan's of Atlanta ensued as did a chain of two hundred steak houses which was to be called the Inner Circle. Ella informed the family that she intended to assume the ownership of substantially more stock than her usual one-ninth in these two hundred steak houses.

VIEUX CARRÉ

RESTAURANT

AIR CONDITIONED

world's greatest tire maker

·DOUBLE EAGLE·
Super-Cushion by
GOOD/YEAR
More people ride on Goodyear tires than on any other kind

Double Eagle, Super-Cushion T. M.—The Goodyear Tire & Rubber Company, Akron, Ohio

Brennan's in a Goodyear ad,
June 1950.

Owen E. Brennan, center, toasting good
friend Curt Gowdy, left, in an ad for
Narragansett Lager Beer.

New Orleans!

Join the party at Brennan's famous French
and Creole Restaurant.
Here Monsieur Brennan did us noble as
you can see. So I added a treat of my own—
'Gansett all round. I brought this great beer
all the way from New England, because I know how
good 'Gansett goes with good food and good friends.
Like always 'Gansett got a salute of approval—for
lightness, dryness and fine flavor. Just shows that folks
everywhere know a good thing when they taste it.

Hi neighbor ... Have a 'Gansett

Curt Gowdy

Curt Gowdy and Narragansett bring you the
Boston Red Sox Games over TV and Radio ... Tune In

Hi Neighbor!

Narragansett LAGER BEER

GANSETT BREWING COMPANY, Cranston, R. I.

"A restaurant is only as good as the last meal served."

O.E.B.

NORMANDIE 12131

LINDSLEY PARSONS PRODUCTIONS, INC.
4376 SUNSET DRIVE
HOLLYWOOD 27, CALIFORNIA

October 22, 1947

Mr. Owen Brennan
The Absinthe House
Bourbon at Bienville
New Orleans, Louisiana

Dear Owen:

I know how you avoid publicity, but I thought that perhaps I might prevail upon you because of our friendship to let us use your name in our forthcoming production entitled CHARLIE CHAN IN NEW ORLEANS. In accordance with the attached copies, please sign them, keep one for your files and return the rest to me.

The picture will be released after the first of the year.

Thanks again for your marvelous hospitality during our recent visit to New Orleans.

Kindest personal regards.

Sincerely,

LINDSLEY PARSONS

LP:sjw
enclosures

JOHN CAMERON SWAYZE

file

March 24, 1953

Dear Mr. Brennan,

Thanks so much for your note.

We had a wonderful meal in your restaurant.

Just the other day I received a card from a friend to whom I had recommended your place. He had just eaten there and enjoyed it a great deal.

All best wishes.

Sincerely,

John Cameron Swayze

NEW YORK 20

NBC NEWS - RCA Bldg. - 30 Rockefeller Plaza,

In July 1973, concerns arose among Maude and her sons regarding the rapid expansion that was occurring. The concerns stemmed from the obvious inability to manage adequately the restaurants that already had been acquired.

The overall quality of the original Brennan's in New Orleans was suffering as were the other acquisitions with the exception of Brennan's Restaurants in Dallas and Houston. Concentration, finances and valued employees had been diverted in the efforts of expansion while culinary excellence was sacrificed.

At the July family meeting in New Orleans, the subject of discontent was first on the agenda. Surprisingly, Ella's panacea was, as she put it, "to split up the corporations and not the family." This may have been possible had everyone agreed to Ella's terms.

*H*owever, after discussing Ella's proposal among themselves, Owen's three sons, Pip, Jimmy and Ted, responded in a manner which Ella probably had not anticipated. Brennan's Restaurant in New Orleans had been their father's legacy for them. Along with their mother, Maude, Pip, Jimmy and Ted controlled its stock and were merely minority stockholders in the six expansion restaurants. These were reasons enough to inform Ella that they would assume sole control of the original Brennan's and that she with her brothers and sisters could have the remaining six expansion restaurants.

"An Associated Press sports article by Joe Reicher and a letter from Owen Brennan arrived at this desk at the same time.

Reicher's tale dealt with an $8 breakfast consumed by Catcher Yogi Berra of the New York Yankees. Brennan's letter contained a hello and the query: 'When you coming to New Orleans again? Haven't seen you in years.'

The letter and story comprised an association of ideas, and revived the memory of a breakfast which made Berra's eight-buck feed seem like an afternoon serving of a hot dog and cup of coffee.

Brennan, proprietor of the famed old Absinthe House and a popular restaurant bearing his name, has a special breakfast which probably isn't duplicated anywhere in this country. Maybe in the world.

The Brennan breakfast, served any time of the day, doesn't bother with such prosaic food as steak, the foundation of Berra's $8 feed."

Alan Ward, Sports Editor,
Oakland Tribune

Intense hours of discussion and negotiations among the accountants and attorneys from both sides of the family ensued for several months following that fateful July meeting. However, no proposal splitting the restaurant corporations equitably was acceptable to Ella as long as she was not awarded the original Brennan's Restaurant. After months of endless negotiations and frustrating attempts to settle this unfortunate family dispute amicably, on November 5, 1973, Maude, Pip, Jimmy and Ted assumed complete control of Brennan's Restaurant of New Orleans resulting in a family schism. The issue of expansion may have been only the tip of the iceberg among the real causes of unrest, unfairness and resentment within the family; but this single issue simplifies the story.

Immediately, after the Brennan family split, Maude, Pip, Jimmy and Ted restored Brennan's to the quality-oriented restaurant that Owen Edward Brennan had originally established. Through the years they have worked diligently to maintain its greatness. Simultaneously, Ella recognized the need to restore Commander's Palace, as it had declined also since its acquisition by the Brennans in 1969. Commander's then provided a New Orleans base for her six restaurant corporations.

Not until November 1974 was a complete and final agreement reached between the two factions of the family. At that time, Maude, Pip, Jimmy and Ted assumed complete ownership of Brennan's Restaurant in New Orleans with no minority stockholders remaining, while Ella and her siblings accomplished the same in all

"…But of all the places we visited and the one that seems to please the most people is Owen Brennan's French Restaurant and Absinthe House. We had a very pleasant chat with Owen, who is known as the 'Happy Irishman,' and his enthusiasm for the welfare of his 'tourists' is contagious. Owen has been very successful. He is a native of the city and is one of its very top businessmen and citizens. One doesn't dare miss Owen's place while in New Orleans."

Ohio Tavern News,
April 10, 1952

Hotel LAST FRONTIER
LAS VEGAS NEVADA

The Early West in Modern Splendor

November 20, 1951

Dear Owen,

Just a note of thanks from both of us for your message. You can be sure the Liberaces will always cherish fond memories of New Orleans.

We are on our way to the Hotel Mapes in Reno, and Palm Springs, the Club Chi Chi during the holiday season.

The Liberace TV show is scheduled for 26 weeks beginning in January, and it will be mid summer of next year before we travel east.

Hope to see you next season when we resume our tour. Until then, our best wishes for your health and happiness.

Always, your friends,

George & "Lee" Liberace

Mr. Owen Brennan
Old Absinthe House
Vieux Carre,
New Orleans, La.

41

MOST LAVISH HOST IN NEW ORLEANS

BY DUANE DECKER

■ ON A HOT afternoon, back in 1933, a discouraged New Orleans businessman named Owen Brennan made an impulsive gesture that was to turn him from a failure into a rather fabulous success.

His discouragement that day stemmed from the fact that his first—and what he guessed was his last—business venture seemed doomed. It was a small neighborhood drugstore which he'd acquired with his modest savings as a door-to-door candy salesman (plus a loan). The drugstore had been in receivership when he'd picked it up and now, under his guidance, it was practically back in receivership.

As he glanced idly through the store window, he noticed eight women waiting at the curb for a bus. They were all Negro domestics, employed by families in the neighborhood, heading home after

a working day. They looked so dejected, so ready to wilt from weariness and heat, that Brennan stopped feeling sorry for himself and began feeling sorry for them.

On impulse, he turned to his soda fountain boy and said: "Make up eight ice cream cones and take them out to those women."

"No charge?" the boy asked, startled.

· "No charge. Tell 'em, compliments of Brennan's."

The impulsive gesture blanked out of Brennan's mind until the next day when an odd series of coincidences began happening. Five neighborhood housewives who had never set foot inside the drugstore before dropped by to make small purchases. Each one let Brennan know that she had come because of a story, related to her by her domestic, about the very generous

112

Pageant Magazine,
April 1954

WILLIAM DUNLAP surveys

The Irish Press,
July 13, 1954

This other Ireland

Owen Brennan

As the result of a kindly act, performed without any thought of reward, Owen Brennan is now one of the richest men in New Orleans.

When he was twenty-three Owen had a drugstore but no customers. He was looking out the window on a hot afternoon, expecting the wolf to come to his door, when he noticed a group of eight women standing at the bus stop.

They were domestics on the way home from work and they were drooping with fatigue. Owen stopped feeling sorry for himself and sent his boy out with eight ice-cream cones for the women.

"No charge," he said. "Tell them, with the compliments of Brennan's."

Owen had five new customers next day. They were neighbourhood housewives. Each woman said she had come into his shop because her domestic had told her about the kindly man who had given out the free ice cream.

ICEMAN COMETH

This gave Owen an idea which was the beginning of a business boom. He hired a couple of boys who scouted the neighbourhood on bicycles watching for new arrivals. When Owen learned that a new family was moving into a house he sent up a carton of ice cream, paper dishes and wooden spoons to coincide with the fuss of the furniture.

"Compliments of Brennan's drugstore," the boy would call out and pedal away cheerfully.

New customers came faster than Owen could count them.

To-day this genial Irishman of forty-three is one of the best known and most popular citizens in the famous French Quarter of New Orleans. Here you have some of the finest restaurants in the world and nowhere is the food better than at the Vieux Carré, run by the man from Ireland.

FATHER SCHUTTEN, MISS ALLEN, BRENNAN
Shamrocks, Shillelaghs Will Be in Order Friday

Owen E. Brennan, far right, as Grand Marshal of the New Orleans St. Patrick's Day Parade.

six expansion restaurants. Since that time, Ella and her brothers and sisters have closed four of their original six restaurants with only Brennan's of Houston and Commander's Palace remaining.

Ella and her family have since expanded their restaurant holdings. Brennan's Restaurant in New Orleans is in no way affiliated with these most recent ventures or any other restaurant operations. Owen's three sons, Pip, Jimmy and Ted, remain the sole owners and operators of their father's world-famous restaurant on Royal Street.

Brennan

Our story and cookbook are dedicated in memory of our father, Owen Edward Brennan, with our deepest appreciation - for without his creativity, determination and dedication where would the Brennan family be today? Had he remained a bookkeeper, perhaps, we all would be accountants. Had he continued his career as a district manager for Schenley, perhaps, we all would be liquor salesmen. Had he owned his own gas station, perhaps, we all would be pumping gas. Had Owen Edward Brennan pursued a different path than he did most probably no Brennan would be where he or she is today. Our father became a successful restaurateur and that conceivably has made any Brennan a restaurateur.

"The best restaurant in the world is the one you are known in."

O.E.B.

Fortunately, for the entire Brennan family, our father pursued his dreams and made them into realities. The misfortune was that fate did not permit him to enjoy those realities for very long. Yet the generations to follow continue to reap the benefits of his success.

In recent years, stories have been written about the Brennan family in which history has been changed. For that reason, our true beginning is so important for the sake of posterity.

We can never forget that it is Owen's spirit of gracious hospitality that we all attempt to emulate today. For it was Owen Edward Brennan who launched his entire family into the restaurant business and not a candy factory. We must remember that Owen's ready wit, radiant smile, infectious laugh, incredible imagination, energy and generosity were the keys to his success. For without these traits and an "Irish smile and a kiss of the Blarney Stone," there never would have been a Brennan's Restaurant.

Pip, Ted and Jimmy Brennan alongside the portrait of their father.

417 ROYAL STREET

⚜

*N*owhere in New Orleans' French Quarter is there a building
with a more illustrious past than 417 Royal Street, the home of
Brennan's Restaurant. Located on the most elegant street of this
historic district and adjacent to some of the finest antique shops in
the world, Brennan's Restaurant has been a landmark on Royal
Street since it first opened on May 31, 1956.

The property was originally given the number 215 by Adrien
de Pauger. In 1721 he designed the original city, now known as
the French Quarter, and assigned lot 215 to Baron Hambourg to
whom it had been granted by the Superior Council.

The first transaction of the Royal Street property on record occurred on
December 3, 1794, when Gaspar Debuys and Huberto Remy purchased
the land from Angela Monget. On December 8, just five days later, the
great fire of 1794 destroyed more than two hundred buildings in the
city, including whatever buildings existed at 417 Royal Street.

During the Spanish rule of Louisiana, Don Vincente Rillieux, the
great-grandfather of the French artist Edgar Dégas, bought the land
from Debuys and Remy. The purchase occurred on January 8, 1795,
exactly one month after the fire. Records show that Debuys and
Remy sold their lot, including the ruins of their building. The lot still
had the original dimensions assigned by Pauger of 60 feet x 120 feet.

The two story structure as we know it today was built by Don Vincente Rillieux in 1795. After Rillieux died, his widow, Dame Maria Fonquet Rillieux, gave the property to her son-in-law, Santiago Freret. On June 2, 1801, Freret relinquished the title to Don José Faurie for 8,650 Mexican pesos.

Faurie not only resided in the handsome new mansion but maintained it as his place of business. On January 26, 1805, Faurie sold his residence to Julien Poydras. As its president, Julien Poydras converted his Royal Street structure into the newly organized Banque de la Louisiane, founded on March 11, 1804, by Governor W.C.C. Claiborne.

The bank was the first financial institution to be operated in New Orleans as well as in all of the territory secured by the United States through the Louisiana Purchase of 1803. Extensive renovations of the building by the bank included the addition of an intricately designed wrought-iron balcony railing with the bank's LB monogram, a compelling example of *ferronnier's* art that still exists within the structure today.

In 1819, after the original Louisiana Bank had outlived its charter, the ground floor of the building was occupied temporarily by the Louisiana State Bank. On October 5, 1820, the liquidators of La Banque de la Louisiane sold the property to Martin Gordon, a socially prominent Virginia gentleman and clerk of the United States District Court.

Opposite: Brennan's carriage entrance.

Brennan's Grand Award-winning wine cellar.

The Gordon family was noted for its lavish hospitality. The family home soon became the center of fashionable Créole social activities. Gordon was active in the politics of the day and a friend of General Andrew Jackson. General Jackson was the guest of honor at many lavish banquets staged at the Gordon home. After Andrew Jackson became President, he appointed Martin Gordon to the office of Collector of the Port of New Orleans in appreciation of Gordon's generosity and hospitality.

Unfortunately, in 1841 the Gordon Family met with financial reverses. The building was seized by the Citizens' Bank and sold at auction by the sheriff. Judge Alonzo Morphy, a former state attorney general and a member of Louisiana's high court, purchased the building.

*J*udge Morphy's son was Paul Charles Morphy, the celebrated American chess master. Known around the world as a young genius, Paul Morphy was only ten years old when he mastered the intricate game. He defeated Europe's foremost chess champions, as newspapers touted his feat of playing eight contestants at one time while blindfolded. Judge Morphy even designed a huge chess board on the floor of one of the upstairs rooms in the mansion for his son's pleasure.

The chess master, Paul Charles Morphy, died in his Royal Street home in 1884. In 1891, his brothers and sisters sold the mansion they had inherited.

The property then passed to several owners, including William Ratcliffe Irby. Irby, who acquired his fortune in tobacco, dairy products and banking, was a member of the Board of Administrators

of Tulane University. He was deeply interested in many philanthropic endeavors and primarily in the preservation of the historic French Quarter. As a result, Irby donated his property at 417 Royal Street to Tulane University in 1920.

Over the years, Tulane University leased the property to a number of tenants. The Patio Royal, a popular spot for debutante parties and other social functions, was the last tenant before its conversion into the world-famous Brennan's Restaurant.

*O*wen Edward Brennan rented the property from Tulane University in 1954. Under the guidance of Owen's architects, Richard Koch and Samuel Wilson, as well as the Vieux Carré Commission, the building was completely renovated.

On April 3, 1975, a raging fire severely damaged and ceased operations at the Royal Street establishment. Amazingly, Brennan's, restored to its original splendor, resumed business in less than six months. Almost ten years later in1984, Owen's three sons, Pip, Jimmy and Ted, purchased the building from Tulane University.

Today the building features twelve elegantly decorated dining rooms, with a total capacity of 550 patrons. What was once the slave quarters of the pre-Civil War mansion has been converted into Brennan's stellar, award-winning wine cellar. Exquisite dining surrounds a romantic patio with huge magnolia trees, lush foliage and a picturesque fountain, while its structure remains one of the most historically significant buildings in the French Quarter.

Opposite: Brennan's patio.

8 large red apples,
     washed and cored

¼ cup plus 3 tablespoons
     sugar

1½ teaspoons cinnamon plus
      extra for dusting

¾ cup water

2 cups heavy cream

1 tablespoon vanilla

Preheat oven to 400 degrees F.

4 Servings

8 hard-boiled eggs

4 romaine lettuce leaves

2 small ripe avocados

12 to 16 ounces Beluga or
    Sevruga Caviar

8 tablespoons parsley,
   finely chopped

2 lemons, halved and
   hollowed out

½ cup sour cream

8 tablespoons capers,
   finely chopped

8 tablespoons onion,
   finely chopped

Toast rounds or melba toast for
garnish

SOUTHERN BAKED APPLE WITH DOUBLE CREAM

Stand the apples upright in a shallow baking pan. In a small bowl, combine ¼ cup sugar and 1½ teaspoons cinnamon. Sprinkle the sugar mixture over the apples, then pour ¾ cup water into the bottom of the pan. Bake the apples in the hot oven for 50 minutes to an hour until very tender.

In a medium bowl, combine the cream, vanilla, and remaining 3 tablespoons sugar. Transfer the baked apples to heated bowls and pour ¼ cup of the cream over each. Dust the apples with cinnamon, then serve.

BELUGA CAVIAR WITH AVOCADO LÉON

Separate the egg whites from the yolks. Finely chop the egg whites and set them aside. Repeat with the egg yolks, keeping them separate from the whites. Peel the avocados and split them in half lengthwise; remove the pits.

Place a romaine lettuce leaf on each of four salad plates. Center an avocado half, pit side up, on the lower half of each plate. Spoon 3 to 4 ounces of caviar into the pit of the avocados. On the upper portion of each plate, arrange in a crescent the following: one-quarter of the chopped egg whites, 2 tablespoons parsley, a halved lemon filled with 2 tablespoons sour cream, 2 tablespoons capers, one-quarter of the chopped egg yolks and 2 tablespoons onion. Garnish the plates with toast rounds and serve.

CRÉOLE CREAM CHEESE EVANGELINE

※

Place the diced fruit in a bowl, cover and refrigerate for 4 hours.

Spoon ½ cup Créole cream cheese into four bowls and top with ½ cup chilled fruit. Drizzle any fruit juice over the cream cheese and serve.

Note: Créole cream cheese is a New Orleans specialty. If unavailable, blend together 12 ounces softened cream cheese, ½ cup sour cream, and 1 tablespoon sugar. Refrigerate for 30 minutes, top with fruit, and serve.

4 Servings

16 ounces (2 cups)
    Créole cream cheese
    (see note)

2 cups diced mixed ripe fruit
    (Oranges, grapes, apples,
    strawberries, cantaloupe,
    honeydew melon, or any
    combination of four fresh
    fruit should be used.)

GRILLED GRAPEFRUIT AU KIRSCH

※

Core the grapefruit, then run a knife inside the rind to loosen the pulp. Top each grapefruit half with 1 tablespoon brown sugar and sprinkle with 1 tablespoon cherry liqueur. Add a pinch of cinnamon to each, then place the grapefruit halves in a shallow pan; broil for 2 to 3 minutes until the sugar melts and the tops brown. If desired, garnish with maraschino cherries and mint leaves. Serve warm.

4 Servings

2 large grapefruit, halved

¼ cup brown sugar

¼ cup cherry liqueur
    (or to taste)

½ teaspoon cinnamon

Maraschino cherries and
    mint leaves for garnish

ASPARAGUS ELLEN

✣

8 Servings

64 *fresh asparagus spears*

2 *cups cold water*

½ *teaspoon salt*

2 *pounds lump crabmeat,*
picked over to remove
any shell and cartilage

¼ *cup (½ stick) butter*

Mousseline sauce
(recipe follows)

Freshly grated Parmesan
cheese for sprinkling

Rinse the asparagus spears thoroughly under cold running water, then trim the stems so that the spears are about 4 inches in length. Using a vegetable peeler or knife, scrape away the tough skin from just below the asparagus tip to the base of the stalk. Place the prepared asparagus in a large sauté pan along with 2 cups of cold water and the salt. Boil the spears gently over medium heat until tender, then remove them from the pan and blot dry on paper towels. Place the cooked asparagus on a warm plate while cooking the crabmeat. Melt the butter in a large skillet. Add the crabmeat and sauté for several minutes until the crabmeat is heated through. To serve, divide the asparagus spears between eight plates. Top the asparagus spears with about ½ cup of crabmeat, then cover with mousseline sauce. Sprinkle with Parmesan cheese and serve hot.

MOUSSELINE SAUCE

✣

½ *cup heavy cream*

Pinch of salt

Pinch of white pepper

1 *teaspoon chopped*
fresh parsley

1 *tablespoon dry white wine*

2 *cups hollandaise sauce*
(see Index)

In a medium bowl, combine the cream, salt, and pepper. Beat the mixture with a whisk until thick enough to form a ribbon trail, then add the parsley, wine, and hollandaise sauce. Fold until thoroughly blended.

BUSTER CRAB PECAN

Clean the crabs by removing the eyes and gills; trim the tails. Sprinkle on both sides with salt and pepper.

Combine the egg and the milk in a shallow bowl and beat until well blended. Dredge the soft-shell crabs in flour, dip them in the egg wash, then redredge them in flour. Melt ¼ cup butter in a large sauté pan over medium heat. Add the crabs to the pan and cook until crisp, about 3 to 4 minutes over medium high heat, turning them once; the crabs are very delicate and should be handled gently during cooking. Remove the crabs from the pan and place them on heated serving plates.

Drain the sauté pan, leaving about 1 tablespoon of pan drippings. Add the pecans to the pan and sauté about 2 minutes. Reduce the heat to low and stir in the Worcestershire and lemon butter sauce. Remove the pan from direct heat until serving.

In a small skillet, melt 2 teaspoons of butter. Add the crabmeat and cook over medium heat for 1 to 2 minutes just until the crabmeat is warmed through; shake the pan or stir gently during cooking, being careful not to break apart the lumps of crabmeat. Top each soft-shell crab with 2 ounces (about ¼ cup) crabmeat, then drizzle with the pecan sauce.

4 Servings

---

1 large egg

¼ cup milk

4 baby soft-shell crabs

All-purpose flour for dredging

¼ cup (½ stick) plus 2 teaspoons butter

1 cup chopped pecans

1 tablespoon Worcestershire sauce

¾ cup lemon butter sauce (see Index)

8 ounces lump crabmeat, picked over to remove any shell and cartilage

Salt and black pepper

BUSTER CRAB VINAIGRETTE

4 Servings

4 baby soft-shell crabs

¼ cup (½ stick) butter

All-purpose flour for dusting

Salt and black pepper

½ cup warm vinaigrette
dressing (see Index)

Clean the crabs by removing the eyes and gills; trim the tails.

Melt the butter in a large sauté pan. Sprinkle the crabs on both sides with salt and pepper, then dust lightly with flour. Place the crabs in the pan and cook over moderately high heat for 3 minutes per side. The crabs are very delicate, so handle them gently during cooking. Place the cooked crabs on heated serving plates and top each with 2 tablespoons vinaigrette dressing.

BUSTER CRAB BÉARNAISE

4 Servings

4 baby soft-shell crabs

¼ cup (½ stick) butter

All-purpose flour for dusting

Salt and black pepper

⅓ cup béarnaise sauce
(see Index)

Clean the crabs by removing the eyes and gills; trim the tails.

Melt the butter in a large sauté pan. Sprinkle the crabs on both sides with salt and pepper, then dust lightly with flour. Place the crabs in the pan and cook over moderately high heat for 3 minutes per side; the crabs are very delicate, so handle them gently during cooking. Place the cooked crabs on heated serving plates and top each with a heaping tablespoon of béarnaise sauce.

CRABMEAT MARINIÈRE

Melt the butter in a small skillet. Add the scallions to the pan and cook for a few minutes over medium heat until tender. Reduce the heat to low, then blend in the flour. Cook the mixture for 3 to 5 minutes, stirring constantly. Pour in the milk and stir until smooth, then add the salt, cayenne, and wine. Simmer 10 minutes, stirring occasionally, then fold in the crabmeat. When the crabmeat is heated through, quickly beat in the egg yolk.

Spoon the crabmeat mixture into four ¾-cup ovenproof molds or ramekins. Sprinkle with paprika, then broil until lightly browned, about 2 to 3 minutes. Serve piping hot.

4 Servings

½	cup (1 stick) butter
1	cup scallions, finely chopped
3	tablespoons all-purpose flour
2	cups milk
½	teaspoon salt
½	teaspoon cayenne pepper
⅓	cup dry white wine
12	ounces lump crabmeat, picked over to remove any shell and cartilage
1	egg yolk, beaten

Paprika for sprinkling

CRÊPE BARBARA

❧

*M*elt the butter over low heat in a large sauté pan, then add the crabmeat and 2 tablespoons water. Season the crabmeat with salt and pepper and cook until heated through, about 5 minutes. Fold in the shrimp and briefly warm the mixture.

Place the crêpes on ovenproof plates. Fill the center of each crêpe with about ¼ cup crabmeat and 2 shrimp. Roll the crêpes and top with ¼ cup hollandaise and 1 tablespoon Parmesan cheese. Broil the crêpes until the cheese melts, about 1 to 2 minutes, and serve immediately.

8 Servings

2	tablespoons butter
1	pound lump crabmeat, picked over to remove any shell and cartilage
2	tablespoons water
16	boiled medium shrimp, peeled and deveined (see Index)

Salt and black pepper

8	crêpes (see Index)
2	cups hollandaise sauce (see Index)
½	cup freshly grated Parmesan cheese

ESCARGOTS BORDELAISE

❧

*C*ombine all of the ingredients, through the white pepper, in the bowl of a food processor. Pulse the machine until the ingredients are well blended. Add salt to taste.

Preheat oven to 425 degrees F.

Fill the bottom of each snail shell with 1 tablespoon of the garlic-flavored butter. Place a snail in each shell, then pack the shells with another tablespoon of garlic butter.

Arrange the shells on a baking sheet that has been sprinkled with water. Bake the snails in the hot oven for 5 to 7 minutes, then divide them between eight small, heated dishes. Serve hot.

8 Servings

1½	pounds (6 sticks) room temperature butter
3	tablespoons minced garlic
½	cup fresh parsley, finely chopped
1½	teaspoons Worcestershire sauce
1	tablespoon (or to taste) Tabasco®
¼	cup brandy
1	teaspoon white pepper

Salt to taste

48 snail shells, washed and drained

48 snails rinsed in warm water

OYSTERS AINSWORTH

$\approx$

$\mathcal{B}$reak apart the Holland rusks and place the pieces in a food processor or blender. Purée the rusks into fine crumbs.

To make the pâté, combine the chicken livers, egg yolks, scallions, and Holland rusk crumbs in a large bowl. Add salt and pepper to taste. Generously butter the bottom and sides of a 1-quart rectangular baking dish. Pour the liver mixture into the dish and set the dish in a larger ovenproof pan; fill the pan with one inch of water. Place the pâté in its water bath in the hot oven and bake for 35 to 40 minutes, until firmly set. Cool the pâté to room temperature, then refrigerate it for several hours until cold.

When the pâté is cold, prepare the oysters. In a shallow bowl or pan, combine the corn flour and cayenne pepper. Season the mixture with salt and pepper. Drain the oysters thoroughly, then dredge them in the seasoned corn flour. Heat oil in a deep fat fryer or large saucepan to 375 degrees F. Fry the oysters in the hot oil until golden brown, about 3 minutes. Drain on paper towels.

Invert the cold pâté onto a plate and cut it into slices.

Divide the toasted bread between four plates. Set a slice of liver pâté on each piece of French bread, top with 3 oysters, then spoon béarnaise sauce over the oysters.

4 Servings

---

6 *Holland rusks*

---

1 *pound chicken livers,*
   finely chopped

---

3 *egg yolks*

⅓ *cup scallions,*
   finely chopped

---

1 *cup corn flour*

¼ *teaspoon cayenne pepper*

---

12 *shucked oysters*

Oil for deep frying

Salt and black pepper

---

4 *slices French bread,*
   cut on the diagonal
   and toasted

½ *cup béarnaise sauce*
   (see Index)

Preheat oven to 375 degrees F.

OYSTERS EDWARD

2 tablespoons butter

4 medium ripe tomatoes,
seeded and minced

1 pound tasso, minced
(see note below)

1½ cups heavy cream

36 oysters in their shells

1 to 1½ cups corn flour

Oil for deep frying

1 cup sour cream

Salt and black pepper

Chopped fresh parsley for
garnish

*M*elt the butter in a medium skillet, then add the tomatoes and sauté them about 3 minutes. Stir in the tasso and cook an additional 3 minutes. Reduce the heat to low and add the whipping cream. Simmer until the sauce thickens, about 6 minutes. Keep the sauce warm until serving.

Using an oyster knife, pry open the oyster shells, then remove the oysters. Discard the top shells; scrub and dry the bottom shells. Drain the oysters.

Place the corn flour in a shallow bowl or pan; season with a pinch each of salt and pepper. Dredge the oysters in the seasoned corn flour, then deep fry them in oil heated to 375 degrees F. until golden brown, about 3 to 4 minutes. Drain on paper towels.

Divide the oyster shells between six large plates or trays.Generously spoon tasso sauce into each oyster shell. Place one fried oyster on top of the sauce. Dot the oysters with a heaping teaspoon of sour cream, garnish with chopped parsley, and serve.

Note: Tasso is highly-seasoned Cajun smoked ham. If unavailable, substitute smoked ham and add cayenne pepper to taste.

Oysters 2-2-2

In the 1950's Owen Edward Brennan created Oysters 2-2-2 or the Three Deuces which offered customers a sampling of two each of Oysters Bienville, Oysters Rockefeller and Oysters Roffignac. The following three recipes comprise this classic dish.

Oysters Bienville

Melt the butter in a 9-inch skillet over medium heat. Add the shrimp, scallions and mushrooms; sauté about 10 minutes until the shrimp turn pink. Sprinkle the flour over the mixture, then stir until blended. Reduce the heat slightly and cook the mixture a couple of minutes, stirring constantly. Do not allow the mixture to scorch.

Remove the pan from the heat and blend in the stock and wine. Season with salt and pepper to taste. When smooth, add the egg yolks, cream and bacon. Return the skillet briefly to low heat, stirring constantly, until the mixture thickens, then add the Worcestershire, parsley and food coloring (if a brighter yellow color is desired). Cook the mixture for 15 minutes, stirring frequently, then set it aside while preparing the oysters.

Using an oyster knife, pry open the oyster shells, then remove the oysters. Discard the top shells; scrub and dry the bottom shells. Drain the oysters. Line four ovenproof pans or trays with a layer of rock salt about an inch deep. Arrange six oyster shells on each tray. Place one oyster in each of the shells.

Spoon the shrimp mixture into a pastry bag fitted with a large plain tip. Pipe (or spoon) a generous amount of shrimp topping onto each oyster, then dust them with Parmesan cheese. Bake in the hot oven for 10 to 12 minutes, until the edges of the oysters begin to curl. Serve each person one tray of hot oysters.

6 tablespoons (¾ stick) butter

1½ cups peeled and deveined shrimp, finely chopped

1 cup scallions, finely chopped

1½ cups mushrooms, finely chopped

1 cup all-purpose flour

1½ cups fish or chicken stock (see Index)

6 tablespoons dry white wine

Salt and pepper to taste

6 egg yolks

1 cup heavy cream

8 ounces bacon, cooked and crumbled

2 tablespoons Worcestershire sauce

1 tablespoon fresh parsley, finely chopped

1 teaspoon eggshade or yellow food coloring (optional)

24 oysters in their shells

Rock salt

Freshly grated Parmesan cheese for garnish

Preheat oven to 350 degrees F.

OYSTERS ROCKEFELLER

8 Servings

---

1 pound (4 sticks) butter

---

1 celery rib, finely chopped

---

2 bunches scallions,
    finely chopped

---

1 bunch parsley,
    finely chopped

---

3 tablespoons
    Worcestershire sauce

---

1 teaspoon Tabasco®

½ to ¾ cup Herbsaint or
    Pernod (use more or
    less according to taste)

1¼ cups seasoned
    bread crumbs

---

48 oysters in their shells

Rock salt

---

*M*elt the butter in a large skillet and add the celery, scallions, and parsley. Sauté for 5 minutes, then add the Worcestershire and Tabasco®. Reduce the heat to medium and cook for 10 minutes. Add the Herbsaint and bread crumbs and cook another 5 minutes. Remove the pan from the heat and transfer the mixture to a bowl. Chill in the refrigerator 1 hour until cold, but not firmly set.

Using an oyster knife, pry open the oyster shells, then remove the oysters. Discard the top shells; scrub and dry the bottom shells. Drain the oysters. Arrange 6 oyster shells on an ovenproof pan or tray lined with a layer of rock salt about an inch deep. Make 8 trays in all. Place 1 oyster in each of the shells.

Preheat oven to 375 degrees F.

Remove the chilled Rockefeller topping from the refrigerator and beat it with an electric mixer to evenly distribute the butter and infuse air into the mixture; transfer the mixture to a pastry bag fitted with a large plain tip.

Pipe a tablespoon of the mixture onto each oyster, then bake in the hot oven for 5 to 8 minutes. Serve each person one tray of piping hot oysters.

OYSTERS ROFFIGNAC

$\mathcal{U}$sing an oyster knife, pry open the oyster shells, then remove the oysters. Reserve any oyster water. Discard the top shells; scrub and dry the bottom shells.

Melt the butter in a medium skillet and sauté the mushrooms, scallions, onion, shrimp, and garlic. When the onion is lightly browned, add the flour, salt, pepper, and cayenne. Cook the mixture over medium heat until the flour begins to brown, about 7 to 10 minutes. Blend in the oyster water and wine; stir until smooth. Reduce the heat to low and simmer for 15 to 20 minutes, stirring occasionally. Remove the mixture from the heat and let cool. Line four ovenproof pans or trays with a layer of rock salt about an inch deep. Arrange six oyster shells on each tray. Set one oyster in each shell. Place the cooked shrimp mixture in a pastry bag fitted with a large plain tip. Pipe the mixture onto the oysters, then bake in the hot oven about 20 minutes, until the edges of the oysters begin to curl. Serve each person one tray of hot oysters.

Note: If the oysters do not yield one cup of oyster water, clam juice can be added.

> "At Bourbon and Bienville Streets in the Vieux Carré in New Orleans is a French restaurant, run by an Irishman named Brennan, who is doing an excellent job. This fine lad has reinstituted the famous French breakfast, along with lots of old French atmosphere and good food. A house specialty is Oysters Roffignac."
>
> Duncan Hines

24 oysters in their shells

¾ cup (1½ sticks) butter

⅓ cup mushrooms, finely chopped

⅓ cup scallions, finely chopped

½ cup onion, finely chopped

½ cup cooked shrimp, finely chopped

2 tablespoons minced garlic

2 tablespoons all-purpose flour

½ teaspoon salt

⅛ teaspoon black pepper

Pinch of cayenne pepper

1 cup oyster water (see note at left)

½ cup red wine

Rock salt

Preheat oven to 400 degrees F.

BAKED OYSTERS CASINO

8 Servings

48	oysters in their shells
12	strips of bacon, lightly cooked and cut into 4 pieces
3	cups cocktail sauce (recipe follows)

Rock salt

Preheat oven to 475 degrees F.

Using an oyster knife, pry open the oyster shells, then remove the oysters. Discard the top shells; scrub and dry the bottom shells. Drain the oysters. Line eight pans or ovenproof trays with a layer of rock salt about an inch deep. Arrange six oyster shells in each pan, then return the oysters to their shells. Top each oyster with a piece of bacon.

Bake the oysters in the oven for three minutes, then remove them from the oven and top each with 1 tablespoon cocktail sauce. Return the oysters to the oven and cook until bubbling hot, about 5 minutes.

Serve each person one tray of oysters.

COCKTAIL SAUCE

In a large bowl, combine the ketchup, chili sauce, and horseradish. Stir in the lemon juice, Worcestershire, salt, and pepper. Chill for at least 2 hours prior to serving.

This sauce will keep, covered, for 2 to 3 weeks in the refrigerator. Cocktail sauce can also be served as a dressing for cold boiled seafood, such as shrimp or crabmeat.

Yields 4 cups

2	cups ketchup
1	cup prepared chili sauce
2½	tablespoons horseradish
1	teaspoon lemon juice
1	teaspoon Worcestershire sauce
½	teaspoon salt
½	teaspoon black pepper

LOUISIANA BOILED SHRIMP

Bring 1 gallon of water to a boil in a stock pot, then add the lemons, bay leaves, cayenne, black pepper, salt, garlic, and crab boil. When the water returns to a boil, add the shrimp. Boil the shrimp for 5 to 8 minutes, then drain in a colander; when cool enough to handle, peel and devein.

6 Servings

1	gallon water
3	large lemons, halved
2	large bay leaves
1½	teaspoons cayenne pepper
1½	teaspoons black pepper
5	tablespoons salt
2	garlic cloves
One 3-ounce bag of crab boil (optional)	
3	pounds medium shrimp

SHRIMP RÉMOULADE

8 Servings

½	cup minced celery
⅓	cup minced scallion tops
⅓	cup minced fresh parsley
¼	cup minced dill pickles
2	tablespoons minced garlic
½	cup Créole mustard
2	teaspoons horseradish (or to taste)
½	cup vegetable oil
¼	cup red wine vinegar
1	tablespoon Worcestershire sauce
	Pinch of salt
	Pinch of white pepper
8	large romaine lettuce leaves
2	cups shredded iceberg lettuce
48	chilled boiled shrimp (see Index)

Combine all of the ingredients, through the white pepper, in a large mixing bowl. Stir until well blended, then chill in the refrigerator for 2 hours.

To serve, place a lettuce leaf on eight plates and top with about ¼ cup shredded lettuce. Arrange 6 boiled shrimp on each plate and drizzle with 2 tablespoons rémoulade sauce.

New Orleans
Barbecued Shrimp

Slice the shrimp lengthwise down the back, being careful not to cut all the way through. Melt the butter in a large skillet and sauté the shrimp for 1 to 2 minutes. Stir in the remaining ingredients and ¼ cup water. Cook briefly, then transfer the shrimp and butter mixture to a shallow ovenproof dish. Bake in the hot oven for 3 to 4 minutes.

To serve, divide the shrimp between four plates, then pour some of the butter sauce over the shrimp. Serve with thinly sliced French bread.

4 Servings

*15 to 20 (about 1 pound)
large shrimp,
peeled and deveined*

½ cup (1 stick) butter

¼ cup water

2 garlic cloves, minced

*1 tablespoon Italian
seasoning*

1 tablespoon thyme leaves

*2 teaspoons chopped
fresh parsley*

1 teaspoon black pepper

Pinch of paprika

Pinch of salt

Pinch of white pepper

Preheat oven to 375 degrees F.

FROG LEGS MEUNIÈRE

4 Servings

1	*large egg*
¼	*cup milk*
8	*pairs of frog legs*
½	*cup all-purpose flour*
1	*cup seasoned bread crumbs*
2	*tablespoons butter*
6	*tablespoons garlic butter (see Index)*
¼	*cup lemon butter sauce (see Index)*

Salt and black pepper

Lemon wedges for garnish

In a shallow bowl or pan, whisk together the egg and milk. Sever the frog legs at the joint and season on both sides with salt and pepper. Coat the legs in flour, dip them in the egg wash, then dredge in bread crumbs.

Heat the butter in a large skillet and fry the frog legs over medium heat for 5 minutes until golden brown on both sides. Remove the legs from the pan and set aside. Drain the skillet, then add the garlic butter; when the pan comes back to temperature, return the frog legs to the pan and cook over medium heat for 5 minutes.

Transfer the frog legs to individual serving plates. Drizzle each plate with some of the garlic butter pan drippings and about 1 tablespoon lemon butter sauce.

CHICKEN LIVER PÂTÉ

*M*elt ½ cup (1 stick) of the butter in a large saucepan. Add the chicken livers, onions, allspice, paprika, salt, and pepper. Cover the pan and simmer the mixture over low heat about 8 minutes.

Transfer the liver mixture to a food processor and purée with the cognac and remaining 3 sticks of butter. Place the purée in a bowl and chill in the refrigerator until partially set, about 30 minutes.

Mold the mixture into a pineapple-shaped loaf and stud the surface with the sliced olives. If desired, cap with a fresh pineapple top. Return the pâté to the refrigerator and chill until firm, then slice and serve with melba toast.

20 Servings

1	pound (4 sticks) butter
2	pounds chicken livers
2	medium onions, quartered
1	teaspoon allspice
1	teaspoon paprika
¼	teaspoon salt
¼	teaspoon black pepper
2	tablespoons cognac
1¼	cups sliced pimento-stuffed olives

Fresh pineapple top (optional)

CRÉOLE LIVER PÂTÉ WITH PECANS

¾ pound calf liver

¾ pound chicken livers

¼ cup cognac

8 white peppercorns, crushed

8 juniper berries, crushed

½ teaspoon ground allspice

1 garlic clove, minced

2 scallions, chopped

¼ cup chopped onion

¼ cup chopped fresh parsley

3 large eggs

½ teaspoon salt

1 teaspoon white pepper

1 cup heavy cream

14 strips of bacon

1 ham steak, ¾ to 1-inch thick, sliced into 4 strips

¾ cup chopped pecans

Cumberland sauce (recipe follows)

In a medium bowl, combine the calf and chicken livers with the cognac, peppercorns, juniper berries, and allspice. Cover the bowl and marinate the liver for 2 hours in the refrigerator.

Preheat oven to 325 degrees F.

Transfer the liver mixture to the bowl of a food processor. Add the garlic, scallions, onion, parsley, eggs, salt, white pepper, and cream, then purée the ingredients. Line a 9 x 5 x 2 ¾-inch loaf pan or 2-quart casserole with the bacon so that the strips overlap the sides of the mold. Pour a third of the liver mixture into the prepared pan. Lay 2 of the ham strips in the mold and sprinkle with half of the chopped pecans. Pour another third of the liver mixture into the mold and add the remaining ham and pecans. Finally, fill the dish with the rest of the puréed liver, fold the bacon over the top to encase the pâté, then place the mold in a larger, shallow pan filled with ½-inch water.

Cut a sheet of parchment paper to fit the pan and set the paper on top of the bacon to keep it from curling during baking. Bake the pâté in its water bath to an internal temperature of 180 degrees, approximately 1 to 1½ hours. After an hour, test the doneness by inserting a knife in the center of the pâté; if the knife comes out clean, the pâté is cooked. Cool the pâté at room temperature, then invert it onto a platter. Transfer the pâté to the refrigerator and chill overnight.

Cut the cold pâté into slices about ½-inch thick. Spoon chilled cumberland sauce over the slices and serve.

CUMBERLAND SAUCE

*M*elt the butter in a saucepan and add the citrus juice and peel and sugar. Cook the mixture over medium heat until the sugar dissolves, then stir in the cranberries and horseradish. Reduce the heat and simmer about 2 minutes. Refrigerate until cold.

1 tablespoon butter

Juice and finely grated peel of 2 lemons

Juice and finely grated peel of 1 orange

1 teaspoon sugar

½ cup jellied cranberries

½ teaspoon horseradish

CORN AND CRAB SOUP

8 Servings

¼ cup (½ stick) butter

1½ cups onion,
   finely chopped

---

2 tablespoons all-purpose
   flour

---

8 cups fresh corn kernels
   (see note below)

1½ quarts (6 cups)
   heavy cream

---

1 pound lump crabmeat,
   picked over to remove
   any shell and cartilage

---

2 tablespoons chopped
   fresh parsley

Salt and white pepper

---

*M*elt the butter in a large saucepan or Dutch oven and sauté the onion until clear and tender. Blend in the flour, then add the corn kernels. Cook the mixture for 5 minutes, stirring frequently. Pour in the cream and season with salt and pepper to taste. Cook over medium heat until the corn is tender, about 20 minutes, stirring occasionally. Add the crabmeat and parsley, cook an additional 5 minutes, then serve.

Note: One large ear of sweet corn yields about 1 cup of corn kernels.

GAZPACHO

❦

*P*our the beef stock into a large bowl, then add the cucumbers, scallions, bell pepper, tomatoes, garlic, tomato juice, red wine vinegar, and Tabasco®. Stir until the ingredients are well combined and season with salt and pepper to taste. Chill in the refrigerator for at least 4 hours, then add the Worcestershire and parsley. Serve the gazpacho in chilled bowls.

Note: For a variation of this popular soup, lump crabmeat or blanched crawfish tails may be added.

6 Servings

2 cups cold beef stock
    (see Index)

2 medium cucumbers,
    peeled, seeded, and
    finely chopped

1 bunch scallions,
    finely chopped

1 medium green bell
    pepper, finely chopped

2 tomatoes, finely chopped

2 garlic cloves, minced

1 cup tomato juice

1 tablespoon
    red wine vinegar

½ teaspoon Tabasco®

2 teaspoons Worcestershire
    sauce

1 teaspoon fresh parsley,
    finely chopped

Salt and black pepper

LOUISIANA CRAB BISQUE

16 Servings

10	pounds (about 20 crabs) live hard-shell crabs, preferably female
1	pound (4 sticks) butter
1	jumbo onion, coarsely chopped
4	celery ribs, coarsely chopped
2	large carrots, coarsely chopped
8	medium tomatoes, quartered
1½	cups chopped parsley
12	garlic cloves, diced
6	bay leaves
12	ounces (1½ cups) tomato paste
2	tablespoons thyme leaves
2	gallons cold water
One	3-ounce bag of crab boil
1	cup dry white wine
8	heaping tablespoons paprika

Clean the crabs by soaking them in tap water about 1 hour. In a 12-quart ovenproof roasting pan, melt 1 cup of the butter then add the onion, celery, carrots, tomatoes, parsley, garlic, bay leaves, tomato paste, and thyme. Stir the mixture together over moderately high heat and cook until hot, about 10 minutes.

Preheat oven to 375 degrees F.

Cover the crabs with a clean towel and, using a mallet, kill and crack the crabs into large pieces. Add the cracked crabs to the roasting pan and cook on top of the stove for 5 minutes, then transfer to the hot oven and roast for 25 minutes, stirring occasionally, until the crabs turn red.

While the crabs are roasting, combine 2 gallons of cold water, the crab boil, wine, paprika, and cayenne in a 24-quart stockpot. Bring the mixture to a boil, then add the contents of the roasting pan. Stir in the saffron and cook for 2 to 3 hours over medium-high heat until reduced to about 1 gallon of stock.

Strain the reduced stock into another large pot and discard the crab pieces and vegetables. Let the stock sit undisturbed for 20 minutes, then strain it through a fine sieve. Next, line the strainer with a single layer of cheesecloth and strain the stock again; repeat this step, then double the thickness of the cheesecloth and strain once more. Strain one final time through a double layer of cheesecloth and let the stock settle for another 20 minutes.

Melt the remaining cup of butter in a medium skillet and blend in the flour. Whisk the mixture over medium heat for 2 to 3 minutes.

Warm the stock over medium heat, then incorporate 6 to 8 tablespoons of the roux into the liquid, whisking until thickened. Stir in the salt, brandy, cream, and crabmeat. Cook the soup until smooth and hot, then serve.

¼ teaspoon cayenne pepper
1½ tablespoons saffron
1¼ cups all-purpose flour
1 teaspoon salt
½ cup brandy
2 cups heavy cream
3 pounds lump crabmeat, picked over to remove any shell and cartilage

CRÉOLE SEAFOOD GUMBO

10 to 12 Servings

¼	cup vegetable oil
1¼	cups all-purpose flour
1	large onion, finely chopped
2	celery ribs, finely chopped
6	garlic cloves, finely chopped
½	green bell pepper, finely chopped
16	ounces (2 cups) tomato sauce
16	ounces (2 cups) canned or very ripe fresh peeled tomatoes
1	pound okra, stemmed and sliced into rings
2	bay leaves
⅓	cup Worcestershire sauce
1½	teaspoons salt
1	teaspoon black pepper
1½	quarts cold water
2	cups (about 48) shucked oysters
4	pounds medium shrimp, peeled and deveined
4	boiled hard-shell crabs, broken in half and gills removed
8	ounces lump crabmeat, picked over to remove any shell and cartilage
1	tablespoon filé powder
5	cups cooked white rice (see Index)

First make a roux by melting the butter in a heavy skillet, then blend in the flour. Cook over a low-medium heat until brown, about 10 – 12 minutes. Add the onion, celery, garlic, and bell pepper and sauté until tender, about 5 minutes. Add the tomato sauce and tomatoes and cook 20 minutes longer. Add the okra, bay leaves, Worcestershire, salt, and pepper, along with 1½ quarts cold water. Cover the pot and cook over medium heat until the okra is tender, about 20 to 30 minutes. Stir in the oysters, shrimp, and crabs, reduce the heat and simmer several minutes until the shrimp are cooked through.

Just before serving, remove the bay leaves and add the lump crabmeat and filé powder. Heat the gumbo briefly, until the crabmeat is warm, then spoon into bowls over hot cooked white rice.

CRÉOLE ONION SOUP

*M*elt the butter in a large pot, and sauté the onion until tender, about 5 minutes. Blend in the flour and cook the mixture over medium heat another 5 minutes, stirring frequently. Add the beef stock, Worcestershire sauce, and pepper. Adjust the seasoning with salt to taste. If desired, add the food coloring. Reduce the heat and simmer until thickened, about 15 minutes. Sprinkle with Parmesan, then serve.

8 Servings

½ cup (1 stick) butter

1 large onion, thinly sliced

½ cup all-purpose flour

2 quarts beef stock (see Index)

2 tablespoons Worcestershire sauce

1 teaspoon white pepper

Salt to taste

2 teaspoons eggshade or yellow food coloring (optional)

¼ cup freshly grated Parmesan cheese

OYSTERS ROCKEFELLER SOUP

6 to 8 Servings

2 cups (about 48)
    shucked oysters

2 quarts cold water

¾ cup (1½ sticks) butter

¾ cup chopped celery

½ cup all-purpose flour

⅓ cup Herbsaint or Pernod

8 ounces fresh spinach
    leaves, washed,
    stemmed, and
    coarsely chopped

¼ cup fresh parsley,
    finely chopped

2 cups heavy cream

Salt and white pepper

*P*lace the oysters in a large saucepan and cover with 2 quarts of cold water. Cook over medium heat just until the oysters begin to curl, about 5 minutes. Strain the oysters, reserving the stock and set them aside.

Melt the butter in a large pot and sauté the celery until tender. Stir in the flour, then add the oysters and oyster stock. Reduce the heat and simmer for 10 minutes until thickened. Add the Herbsaint, spinach, and parsley; season to taste with salt and pepper. Pour in the cream and simmer several minutes until the soup is hot, then serve.

OYSTER SOUP BRENNAN

*I*n a large saucepan, combine the oysters and 3 quarts cold water. Bring the water to a boil, then reduce the heat and simmer about 5 minutes; skim any residue from the surface. Strain the oysters, reserving the stock. Dice the oysters and set aside. Melt the butter in a large pot and sauté the celery and garlic over medium heat about 5 minutes until tender. Add the scallions, bay leaves, and thyme, then stir in the flour. Cook the mixture for 5 minutes over low heat, stirring constantly. Using a whisk, blend in the oyster stock, then add the Worcestershire, salt, and pepper. Cook the soup over medium heat about 20 minutes until thickened, then add the parsley and oysters. Simmer until the oysters are warmed through, about 5 minutes. Remove the bay leaves before serving.

10 to 12 Servings

2	cups (about 48) shucked oysters
3	quarts cold water
¾	cup (1½ sticks) butter
1	cup celery, finely chopped
1½	tablespoons garlic, finely chopped
1	cup scallions, finely chopped
4	bay leaves
1	tablespoon thyme leaves
1	cup all-purpose flour
1½	tablespoons Worcestershire sauce
1	teaspoon salt
1	teaspoon white pepper
½	cup fresh parsley, finely chopped

CHICKEN ANDOUILLE GUMBO

✲

8 to 10 servings

---

1 whole chicken, about 2½
to 3 pounds

⅓ cup vegetable oil

¾ cup all-purpose flour

1 cup diced green bell pepper

1 cup diced onion

1 cup diced celery

2 cups thinly sliced
andouille or other spicy
smoked sausage

4 ripe tomatoes, seeded and
chopped

2 quarts chicken stock
(see Index)

1 teaspoon thyme leaves

4 bay leaves

1 teaspoon black pepper

1 teaspoon garlic,
finely chopped

1 tablespoon filé powder

¼ teaspoon cayenne pepper

Salt to taste

3 cups sliced okra

1 cup cooked white rice
(see Index)

Preheat oven to 350 degrees F.

*R*inse the chicken under cold water and cut it into 10 pieces; halve the breasts, for a total of 12 pieces. Place the chicken pieces, skin side down, in a large ovenproof skillet. Roast the chicken in the hot oven for 20 to 30 minutes until brown.

While the chicken is browning, combine the oil and flour in a 3-quart pot. Cook over medium heat, stirring constantly, until the mixture turns chestnut brown; watch the mixture carefully and do not allow it to burn. Add the bell pepper, onion and celery, and cook the vegetables over medium-high heat until tender. Stir in the andouille and tomatoes; when well combined, pour in the chicken stock. Add the thyme, bay leaves, black pepper and garlic, then using a whisk, stir the filé into the gumbo. Bring the mixture to a boil, then add the cayenne. Adjust the seasoning with salt to taste.

Remove the chicken from the oven and pour off the fat. Reduce the heat under the gumbo to low, then add the chicken and okra. Simmer for 20 to 30 minutes until the okra is tender, then spoon the gumbo into bowls containing about a tablespoon of hot cooked white rice.

RED BEAN GUMBO

8 Servings

*P*lace the beans in a stockpot and add 10 cups cold water. Bring the beans to a boil over high heat, then reduce the heat to medium and cook for 10 minutes. Add the onion, celery, bell pepper, garlic, bacon, tasso, thyme, and filé. Cook the mixture, loosely covered, at a low boil about 1½ hours until the beans begin to break apart; stir frequently. Purée two-thirds of the bean mixture in a food processor or mash through a fine sieve. Pour the bean purée into a large pot and add the oysters, shrimp, and remaining third of the cooked beans. Simmer the soup for 5 minutes, then stir in the crabmeat. Season the gumbo with salt and pepper to taste, then serve over warm cooked white rice.

Note: Tasso is highly-seasoned Cajun smoked ham. If unavailable, substitute smoked ham and add cayenne pepper to taste.

1	pound red kidney beans
10	cups cold water
1	cup diced onion
1	cup diced celery
1	cup diced green bell pepper
1	tablespoon chopped garlic
6	strips of bacon, diced
1½	cups diced tasso (see note below)
1	tablespoon thyme leaves
1	tablespoon filé powder
32	shucked oysters
1	pound peeled and deveined medium shrimp
1	pound lump crabmeat, picked over to remove any shell and cartilage
	Salt and black pepper
4	cups cooked white rice (see Index)

HIS MAJESTY'S OYSTER STEW

6 Servings

4	tablespoons (½ stick) butter
36	shucked oysters
1	tablespoon Worcestershire sauce
3	cups heavy cream
1	cup milk
¼	teaspoon white pepper
¼	teaspoon Tabasco®
Salt to taste	

*M*elt 2 tablespoons of the butter in a large saucepan, then sauté the oysters a couple of minutes until the edges begin to curl. Add the Worcestershire, cream, and milk. Reduce the heat and simmer for 15 to 20 minutes until the soup is hot; do not allow the liquid to reach a boil. Just before serving, add the white pepper, Tabasco®, and remaining 2 tablespoons butter. Adjust the seasoning with salt to taste.

RED BEAN SOUP

6 Servings

1	cup red kidney beans
1	cup (2 sticks) butter
1	cup chopped onion
1	cup chopped celery
1	tablespoon chopped garlic
½	cup all-purpose flour
6	cups beef stock (see Index)
½	teaspoon black pepper
Salt	

*R*inse the kidney beans, then place them in a medium bowl and add water to cover. Soak the beans overnight; drain before preparing the soup.

Melt the butter in a large saucepan or Dutch oven and sauté the onion, celery, and garlic for 10 minutes. Blend in the flour and cook for 1 to 2 minutes, stirring constantly. Add the beef stock and beans, then cook at a low boil for 1½ to 2 hours until the beans are very tender. Strain the soup in a fine sieve, mashing the beans through the strainer. Reheat the soup, adding the pepper. Season with salt to taste and serve.

CHILLED SALMON BISQUE

*M*elt 2 tablespoons of the butter in a medium skillet and sauté the onion, bell pepper, and garlic until tender. Remove the vegetables from the heat and set aside.

In a large saucepan, heat the milk and chopped dill to just under a boil. Season the salmon fillets on both sides with salt and pepper, then poach them in the simmering milk until flaky, about 10 minutes. Transfer the salmon along with the milk to the bowl of a food processor. Purée the salmon, then add the cream and the remaining tablespoon of butter. When the mixture is smooth, add the sautéed vegetables and purée with the salmon. Pour the soup into a stainless steel bowl, then stir in the sherry and cayenne. Season to taste with salt and white pepper, cover the bowl and refrigerate for 1 to 2 hours until chilled.

Spoon the salmon bisque into chilled bowls and garnish with fresh dill.

4 to 6 Servings

3	tablespoons butter
1	small onion, sliced
½	green bell pepper, chopped
1	garlic clove, minced
1½	cups milk
1	tablespoon fresh dill, finely chopped
4	salmon fillets, about 6 ounces each
¾	cup heavy cream
2	tablespoons sherry
½	teaspoon cayenne pepper

Salt and white pepper

Dill sprigs for garnish

New Orleans Turtle Soup

10 to 12 Servings

3 pounds turtle meat

2 bay leaves

2 tablespoons plus
   1 teaspoon salt

4 quarts cold water

½ cup (1 stick) butter

½ cup onion, finely chopped

½ cup celery, finely chopped

½ cup green bell pepper,
   finely chopped

½ teaspoon garlic, minced

1 cup fresh parsley,
   finely chopped

4 ounces (½ cup)
   tomato paste

1 teaspoon caramel
   coloring (optional)

¼ cup Worcestershire sauce

1 teaspoon black pepper

1 teaspoon paprika

1 cup all-purpose flour

3 large hard-boiled eggs,
   finely chopped

1 cup sherry

1 lemon, thinly sliced

*I*n a stockpot, combine the turtle meat, bay leaves, and 2 tablespoons of the salt. Add 4 quarts of cold water and bring the mixture to a boil over high heat. Reduce the heat to medium and cook until the turtle meat is tender, about 2 hours; add additional water, if necessary, to maintain about 3 quarts of liquid during cooking. Strain the turtle meat, reserving the stock. Dice the turtle meat and set aside.

In a large pot, melt the butter and add the onion, celery, bell pepper, garlic, parsley, tomato paste, caramel coloring, Worcestershire, pepper, paprika, and remaining teaspoon of salt. Cook the mixture over low heat until the vegetables are very tender, then stir in the flour. Increase the heat to medium and cook until the flour absorbs all of the butter. Pour the turtle stock into the pot and bring the stock to a boil. Add the turtle meat and simmer for 30 to 40 minutes. Just before serving, remove the bay leaves and add the chopped eggs, sherry, and lemon.

VICHYSSOISE VIEUX CARRÉ

Place the potatoes, ham, onion, and celery in a large pot and add water to cover. Bring the mixture to a boil, then cook over medium heat until the potatoes are very tender, about 20 minutes. Remove the potato mixture from the heat and pour off the excess water. Cream the mixture with a fork or potato masher, then strain in a fine sieve, mashing the potatoes through the strainer. To the strained potatoes, add the cream, milk, shallots, Worcestershire, and peppers. Adjust the seasoning with salt to taste, then chill for 3 to 4 hours.

Serve the vichyssoise in chilled bowls, garnished with chopped parsley.

8 to 10 Servings

5 large Idaho potatoes, peeled and thinly sliced
¾ cup diced boiled ham
1 large onion, thinly sliced
1 cup chopped celery
1 cup heavy cream
2 cups milk
½ cup chopped shallots
1 tablespoon Worcestershire sauce
Pinch of cayenne pepper
Pinch of white pepper
Salt to taste
Chopped fresh parsley for garnish

BEEF STOCK

Yields 2 quarts

1	pound beef bones
1	small white onion, diced
1	celery rib, diced
1	carrot, diced
1	garlic clove
½	bunch scallions, diced
4	quarts cold water

Preheat oven to 450 degrees F.

*A*rrange the beef bones in a single layer in a roasting pan. Roast in a hot oven until brown, about 15 minutes, stirring the bones occasionally.

Transfer the bones to a stockpot and add the remaining ingredients; cover with 4 quarts cold water. Bring the stock to a boil over high heat, skimming away the scum from the surface. Lower the heat and cook at a low rolling boil until reduced by half, about 2 hours. Strain and use immediately or freeze in smaller portions for use in a variety of recipes.

CHICKEN STOCK

Combine all the ingredients in a stockpot and cover with 3 quarts cold water. Bring the stock to a boil over high heat, skimming away the scum that rises to the surface. Reduce the heat and cook at a low rolling boil until reduced by half, about 2 hours. Strain the stock and use immediately or cover and refrigerate. Chicken stock can be frozen in smaller quantities for use in a variety of recipes.

Yields 1½ quarts

3	pounds chicken bones and parts
1	small onion, diced
1	carrot, diced
1	celery rib, diced
1	garlic clove
3	quarts cold water

FISH STOCK

Bring 1½ quarts of cold water to a boil in a large saucepan, along with the lemon and white wine. When the water reaches a rolling boil, add the fish bones and trimmings. Lower the heat and simmer until reduced by half, about 2 hours. Drain and refrigerate, covered, for several days or freeze for future use.

Yields 3 cups

1½	quarts cold water
1	pound fish bones and trimmings
½	of a lemon
½	cup dry white wine

BRENNAN'S BÉARNAISE SAUCE

Yields 2 cups

1 pound butter

4 egg yolks

1½ teaspoons red wine
vinegar

Pinch of cayenne pepper

1 teaspoon salt

1½ teaspoons water

1 tablespoon tarragon
vinegar

1 tablespoon dry white wine

1 tablespoon shallots,
finely chopped

1 tablespoon capers,
drained

1 tablespoon chopped fresh
parsley

*M*elt the butter in a medium saucepan; skim and discard the milk solids from the top of the butter. Hold the clarified butter over very low heat while preparing the egg yolks.

Place the egg yolks, vinegar, cayenne, and salt in a large stainless steel bowl and whisk briefly. Fill a saucepan or Dutch oven large enough to accommodate the bowl with about 1 inch of water. Heat the water to just below the boiling point. Set the bowl in the pan over the water; do not let the water touch the bottom of the bowl. Whisk the egg yolk mixture until slightly thickened, then drizzle the clarified butter into the yolks, whisking constantly. If the bottom of the bowl becomes hotter than warm to the touch, remove the bowl from the pan of water for a few seconds and let cool. When all of the butter is incorporated and the sauce is thick, beat in the water. Fold in the vinegar, wine, shallots, capers, and parsley.

Serve the béarnaise immediately or keep in a warm place at room temperature until use.

Brown Sauce

Melt the butter in a large saucepan. Blend in the flour, then add the remaining ingredients and stir until smooth. Cook over medium heat until the sauce thickens, about 10 to 15 minutes.

Brown sauce appears in a variety of seafood and meat dishes. It can be frozen in ½ or 1 cup portions for use as a base for lemon butter and other sauces.

Yields 2 cups

3	tablespoons butter
3	tablespoons all-purpose flour
1	tablespoon tomato paste
1	tablespoon Worcestershire sauce
2	tablespoons prepared steak sauce
2	cups beef stock (see Index)

Créole Brown Roux

Melt the butter in a heavy skillet, then blend in the flour. Cook the mixture slowly over low heat, stirring frequently, until the roux changes from blonde to brown in color.

Use the roux immediately or freeze in tablespoons. Sealed in plastic, the frozen roux will keep for several months.

¼	cup (½ stick) butter (Vegetable oil or pan drippings can be substituted.)
1¼	cup all-purpose flour

CRÉOLE SAUCE

Yields 1½ quarts

½ cup (1 stick) butter
1½ cups chopped green bell pepper
1½ cups chopped onion
1½ cups chopped celery
1 tablespoon garlic, finely chopped
¼ cup tomato paste
2 tablespoons paprika
1½ teaspoons Italian seasoning
1½ cups chicken stock or water
1 cup tomato juice
1 cup peeled and chopped tomatoes
1½ teaspoons Worcestershire sauce
1½ teaspoons salt
Pinch of black pepper
Pinch of cayenne pepper
Pinch of white pepper
1½ tablespoons cornstarch
4 tablespoons water
¼ chopped fresh parsley

*M*elt the butter in a large saucepan and cook the bell pepper, onion, celery, and garlic until tender, 5 to 8 minutes. Stir in the tomato paste, paprika, and Italian seasoning and cook an additional 3 minutes. Add 1½ cups chicken stock or water, tomato juice, tomatoes, Worcestershire, salt, black, cayenne, and white pepper. Bring the mixture to a boil, then reduce the heat and simmer for 8 to 10 minutes, stirring frequently.

In a small bowl, blend the cornstarch with 4 tablespoons water until smooth. Gradually add the cornstarch to the mixture, stirring constantly, until the sauce thickens. Sprinkle with parsley and serve.

Use Créole sauce immediately or freeze indefinitely.

HOLLANDAISE SAUCE

❧

$\mathcal{M}$elt the butter in a medium saucepan; skim and discard the milk solids from the top of the butter. Hold the clarified butter over very low heat while preparing the egg yolks.

Place the egg yolks, vinegar, cayenne, and salt in a large stainless steel bowl and whisk briefly. Fill a saucepan or Dutch oven large enough to accommodate the bowl with about 1 inch of water. Heat the water to just below the boiling point. Set the bowl in the pan over the water; do not let the water touch the bottom of the bowl. Whisk the egg yolk mixture until slightly thickened, then drizzle the clarified butter into the yolks, whisking constantly. If the bottom of the bowl becomes hotter than warm to the touch, remove the bowl from the pan of water for a few seconds and let cool. When all of the butter is incorporated and the sauce is thick, beat in the water.

Serve the hollandaise immediately or keep in a warm place at room temperature until use.

Yields 2 cups

1	pound butter
4	egg yolks
1½	teaspoons red wine vinegar

Pinch of cayenne pepper

1	teaspoon salt
1½	teaspoons water

LEMON BUTTER SAUCE

✤

Yields 4 cups

$\frac{1}{2}$ *cup brown sauce*
(see Index)

$\frac{1}{4}$ *to* $\frac{1}{2}$ *cup lemon juice*

---

2 *pounds butter,*
room temperature

---

*C*ombine the brown sauce and ¼ cup lemon juice in a large saucepan. Working the pan on and off direct heat, add the butter a bit at a time, whisking the sauce smooth between additions. Add additional lemon juice according to taste.

When all of the butter is incorporated, transfer the sauce to another pan or bowl, and hold at room temperature until serving.

GARLIC BUTTER

✤

Yields $\frac{1}{2}$ *cup*

$\frac{1}{2}$ *cup (1 stick) room*
temperature butter

---

1 *teaspoon Worcestershire*
sauce

---

1 *tablespoon brandy*

---

3 *garlic cloves, minced*

---

1 *teaspoon fresh parsley,*
finely chopped

---

1 *teaspoon Tabasco®*

Pinch of salt

---

*C*ombine all of the ingredients in a small bowl and blend thoroughly.

Marchand De Vin Sauce

Melt the butter in a large saucepan or Dutch oven and sauté the onion, garlic, scallions, and ham for 5 minutes. Add the mushrooms, reduce the heat to medium and cook for 2 minutes. Blend in the flour and cook, stirring, for 4 minutes, then add the Worcestershire, beef stock, wine, thyme, and bay leaf. Simmer until the sauce thickens, about 1 hour. Before serving, remove the bay leaf and add the parsley. Season with salt and pepper to taste.

Yields 3 cups

6	tablespoons butter
½	cup onion, finely chopped
1½	teaspoons garlic, finely chopped
½	cup scallions, finely chopped
½	cup boiled ham, finely chopped
½	cup mushrooms, finely chopped
⅓	cup all-purpose flour
2	tablespoons Worcestershire sauce
2	cups beef stock (see Index)
½	cup red wine
1½	teaspoons thyme leaves
1	bay leaf
½	cup fresh parsley, finely chopped
	Salt and black pepper

PEPPER SAUCE

Yields 2 cups

1	tablespoon butter
1	tablespoon all-purpose flour
1	cup beef stock (see Index)
½	teaspoon tomato paste
1	cup heavy cream
1	teaspoon cracked peppercorns
2	tablespoons brandy

*M*elt the butter in a medium sauté pan. Using a whisk, blend in the flour, then add the beef stock and tomato paste. Cook the mixture over medium heat for 3 to 4 minutes. Add the cream and peppercorns and simmer the sauce until thickened, about 5 minutes. Stir in the brandy and serve immediately.

BRENNAN'S RED WINE AND MUSHROOM SAUCE

❧

*I*n a large saucepan or Dutch oven, melt the butter. Add the onions and sauté for several minutes until tender. Stir in the tomato paste, mushrooms, and paprika; cook until the mushrooms are tender, then add the flour. Stir the mixture until well blended, then using a whisk, incorporate the beef stock. When the sauce is smooth, add the scallions, Worcestershire, wine, and garlic. Season with salt and pepper and simmer about 25 minutes. Serve warm.

Yields 3 cups

½ cup (1 stick) butter

1 cup diced onion

4 ounces (½ cup) tomato paste

2 cups sliced mushrooms

1½ tablespoons paprika

¼ cup all-purpose flour

3 cups beef stock (see Index)

2 cups sliced scallions

1 tablespoon Worcestershire sauce

¾ cup Burgundy wine

1 tablespoon minced garlic

Salt and black pepper

SALADS AND SALAD DRESSINGS

WARM STUFFED ARTICHOKE VINAIGRETTE

❧

4 Entrée Servings

---

4 *medium artichokes*

2 *lemons, halved*

¼ *cup chopped celery*

4 *garlic cloves*

1 *teaspoon white pepper*

3 *tablespoons butter*

1 *pound medium shrimp, peeled and deveined*

1 *tablespoon chopped fresh parsley*

Salt and black pepper

1 *pound angel hair pasta*

2 *cups warm vinaigrette dressing (see Index)*

*W*ash the artichokes, then remove the stems and trim the sharp points from the leaves.

Fill a large pot three-quarters full with cold water. To the water, add the lemon, celery, garlic, white pepper, and a pinch each of salt and black pepper. Bring the water to a boil, then stand the artichokes upright in the pan; place a plate or other weight on top of the artichokes to keep them in position during cooking. Cook the artichokes at a rolling boil until tender, about 50 minutes. Remove the artichokes from the water, drain them, and let cool. When cool enough to handle, spread open the artichokes from the top and remove the furry choke, exposing the heart.

Melt the butter in a skillet and add the shrimp. Season the shrimp with a pinch of salt and pepper, and sprinkle with parsley. Sauté the shrimp a few minutes, until they turn pink, then remove them from the heat.

Boil the pasta until tender, 5 to 7 minutes, then drain and toss with the shrimp.

Fill the centers of the artichokes with the shrimp and pasta. Spoon warm vinaigrette over the artichokes and serve immediately.

Brennan's
Blackened Redfish Salad

6 Entrée Servings

*I*n a small bowl, combine the cayenne, black pepper, 1 tablespoon of the white pepper, and ½ teaspoon of the salt (or less according to taste). Set the seasoning mixture aside.

Place the redfish in a shallow dish and pour the Worcestershire sauce over the fillets. Marinate the fish for 30 minutes in the refrigerator, turning the fish several times.

In a medium bowl or cruet, combine the peanut oil and vinegar with the remaining ½ teaspoon of white pepper and 1 teaspoon salt. Whisk until well blended, then set the dressing aside.
Preheat oven to 350 degrees F.
Spread the pecans in a single layer on a rimmed baking sheet and roast in the hot oven about 8 minutes. Let cool.

Sprinkle the marinated fillets on both sides with the seasoning mixture. Coat a large cast iron skillet with the oil and heat until almost smoking. Place the redfish in the hot skillet and sear about 2 minutes per side, until the seasoning mixture has melted into the fish. Remove from the skillet and break or cut into bite-size pieces.

In a large bowl, combine the romaine, scallions, endive, and blackened redfish. Add dressing as desired and toss until the ingredients are well coated.

Mound blackened redfish salad on six chilled plates and garnish with roasted pecans.

1	tablespoon cayenne pepper
1	tablespoon black pepper
1	tablespoon plus ½ teaspoon white pepper
1½	teaspoons salt
6	redfish fillets, 6 to 8 ounces each (Tilapia, drum or trout can be substituted.)
1	cup Worcestershire sauce
1¼	cups peanut oil
1¼	cups red wine vinegar
1½	cups chopped pecans
1	tablespoon vegetable oil
3	heads romaine lettuce, chopped into bite-size pieces
1½	cups chopped scallions
3	heads Belgian endive, sliced diagonally

BRENNAN SALAD

4 Servings

1 head romaine lettuce
1 cup croutons
¼ cup freshly grated Parmesan cheese
1 cup Brennan dressing (see Index)

Wash the romaine and set aside 4 large leaves. Chop the remaining leaves into 1-inch pieces and place the greens in a salad bowl. Add the croutons and Parmesan, then toss gently. Pour the dressing over the salad and toss again.

To serve, place the lettuce leaves on four chilled plates and mound salad in the center of each leaf.

BRENNAN SEAFOOD SALAD

4 Entrée Servings

1 head romaine lettuce
8 ounces lump crabmeat, picked over to remove any shell and cartilage
8 ounces boiled shrimp, peeled and deveined (see Index)
1½ cups croutons
1 cup freshly grated Parmesan cheese
1 cup Brennan dressing (see Index)

Wash the romaine and set aside 4 large leaves. Chop the remaining leaves into bite-size pieces and place in a large bowl with the crabmeat, shrimp, croutons, and Parmesan. Toss the ingredients, then pour the dressing over the salad and toss again.

Line four plates with lettuce leaves, then top with salad. If desired, garnish with cherry tomatoes and slices of hard-boiled eggs.

GRILLED CHICKEN CAESAR SALAD

❦

Wash the romaine lettuce and chop the leaves into bite-size pieces. Place the chopped lettuce in a large bowl.

Season the chicken breasts on both sides with salt and pepper, then grill or broil the chicken until completely cooked, about 5 to 7 minutes per side. Cut the breasts into bite-size pieces and add the pieces to the bowl with the Romaine lettuce. Add the croutons, then toss the salad.

Pour the Caesar dressing over the salad and toss until the ingredients are well coated. Mound the salad onto six chilled plates and sprinkle with Romano cheese. If desired, garnish with cherry tomatoes, wedges of boiled egg, radishes, carrots, or assorted pickled vegetables.

Note: 6 salmon fillets, about 6 to 8 ounces each, can be substituted for the chicken.

6 Entrée Servings

3	*heads romaine lettuce*
6	*whole boneless, skinless chicken breasts (see note below)*
6	*cups croutons*
3	*cups Caesar dressing (see Index)*
1	*cup freshly grated Romano cheese*
	Salt and black pepper

Preheat a grill or broiler.

CHICKEN ESPLANADE

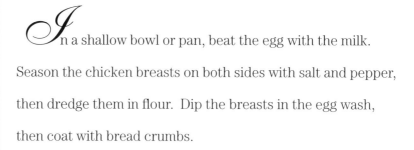

4 Entrée Servings

---

1 *large egg*

¼ cup milk

---

4 *whole boneless,*
   skinless chicken breasts
   (see note below)

All-purpose flour for dredging

---

1 *cup seasoned*
   bread crumbs

¼ cup (½ stick) butter

Salt and black pepper

Brennan salad (see Index)

---

2 *cups grillade sauce*
   (see Index)

$\mathscr{I}$n a shallow bowl or pan, beat the egg with the milk.
Season the chicken breasts on both sides with salt and pepper,
then dredge them in flour. Dip the breasts in the egg wash,
then coat with bread crumbs.

Melt the butter in a large sauté pan and cook the breasts over
moderately high heat about 5 minutes per side until golden brown
and crispy.

Mound a bed of Brennan's salad on four plates. Slice the chicken
breasts and arrange the strips on top of the salad. Spoon grillade
sauce over the chicken and serve.

Note: Four lightly pounded veal escalopes, 4 to 6 ounces each, can
be substituted for the chicken.

CHICKEN SALAD THÉODORE

Season the chicken breasts with 1 teaspoon of the white pepper, then grill or broil until fully cooked, about 5 to 7 minutes per side. Refrigerate the cooked breasts until cold, then chop them into a large dice.

Place the diced chicken in a large bowl and combine with the celery, scallions, shallots, mayonnaise, mustard, remaining white pepper, and parsley. Mix well and chill completely before serving.

Spread the pecans on a pie pan and toast about 5 minutes in an oven preheated to 300 degrees F. Let cool.

Arrange a bed of shredded lettuce on six chilled serving plates. For each serving, pack salad into a 1-cup mold, then invert onto the lettuce beds. Garnish with apple slices and strawberries. Sprinkle each salad with toasted pecans and serve.

6 Entrée Servings

6	whole boneless, skinless chicken breasts
2	teaspoons white pepper
1	cup celery, finely chopped
½	cup scallions, finely chopped
⅓	cup shallots, finely chopped
¾	cup mayonnaise (see Index)
¼	cup Dijon mustard
¼	cup chopped fresh parsley
½	cup chopped pecans
1	head iceberg lettuce, shredded
1	red delicious apple, thinly sliced
1	pint strawberries, stemmed and halved

Preheat a grill or broiler.

COBB SALAD

4 Entrée Servings

4	whole boneless, skinless chicken breasts
2	tablespoons butter
1½	cups chicken stock (see Index)
1	head iceberg lettuce
2	tomatoes, diced
¼	cup crumbled cooked bacon
¼	cup crumbled bleu cheese
2	avocados, diced
1⅓	cups French dressing (see Index)
1	teaspoon minced garlic
Salt and black pepper	

Season the chicken breasts with salt and pepper. Combine the butter and chicken stock in a large sauté pan and heat the stock to just below the boiling point. Place the chicken breasts in the hot stock and poach for 15 to 20 minutes until the chicken is cooked through. Remove the chicken breasts from the stock and cut into a large dice.

Wash the lettuce and set aside four large leaves. Chop the remaining lettuce into bite-size pieces.

In a large bowl combine the chicken with the chopped lettuce, tomatoes, bacon, bleu cheese, and avocado. Toss the ingredients together, then add the French dressing and garlic and toss again.

Serve the salad on chilled plates lined with lettuce leaves.

CRABMEAT BOURGEOIS

❧

*T*rim the lower part of the asparagus spears, then remove the woody skin with a peeler. Steam the asparagus about 12 minutes until tender. Refrigerate the spears until cold.

Place the lettuce leaves on four chilled plates. Mound ½ cup shredded lettuce on the leaves, then arrange 6 asparagus spears radiating out from the center of each plate, with the tips toward the edge of the plate. Set a tomato slice in the center, then top with crabmeat and onion. Spoon 2 tablespoons of French dressing over the crabmeat and garnish with chives.

4 Servings

24	*fresh asparagus spears*
4	*large lettuce leaves*
2	*cups shredded lettuce*
4	*thin slices ripe tomato*
12	*ounces lump crabmeat, picked over to remove any shell and cartilage*
¼	*cup onion, finely chopped*
½	*cup French dressing (see Index)*

Chopped chives for garnish

DUCK BREAST SALAD

✤

6 Entrée Servings

---

3   *cups balsamic vinegar*

¾   *cup walnut oil*
    (Peanut oil can
    be substituted.)

---

5   *teaspoons green*
    peppercorns

---

1   *cup sliced red onion*

---

5   *teaspoons chopped garlic*

¾   *teaspoon salt*

---

6   *skinless duck breasts,*
    about 6 to 8 ounces
    each

---

3   *heads romaine lettuce,*
    chopped into
    bite-size pieces

---

*I*n a large bowl, combine the balsamic vinegar, walnut oil, green peppercorns, onion, garlic, and salt.

Place the duck breasts in a single layer in a shallow dish and cover with the vinegar mixture. Marinate in the refrigerator for 2 hours, turning the breasts once.

Preheat a grill or broiler.

Remove the duck from the marinade and grill or broil about 10 minutes until medium rare. Let the breasts cool for 10 minutes, then cut them on the diagonal into thin slices. While the duck is cooling, place the marinade, along with any juices from the duck, in a saucepan and reduce by a third.

Mound a bed of chopped romaine on six plates and fan slices of duck on top of the lettuce. Spoon the reduced marinade over each salad and serve.

Hearts of Palm Vinaigrette

*W*ash and core the lettuce. Reserve 4 large leaves for presentation; shred the remaining lettuce. Slice the hearts of palm in half lengthwise.

Line four chilled plates with large leaves, then top with shredded lettuce and sliced hearts of palm. Spoon vinaigrette over each salad and garnish with black olives and cherry tomatoes.

4 Servings

1	small head iceberg lettuce
15½	ounces (about 8) hearts of palm, chilled
1⅓	cups chilled vinaigrette dressing (see Index)
8	black olives
8	cherry tomatoes

Jackson Salad

*W*ash and core the lettuce. Reserve 4 large leaves for presentation; chop the remaining lettuce into bite-size pieces.

Place the chopped lettuce into a large bowl with the eggs, chives, bacon, and bleu cheese. Toss the ingredients, then add the French and bleu cheese dressings. Toss the salad until well coated with dressing, then mound on chilled plates lined with lettuce leaves.

8 Servings

2	heads iceberg lettuce
4	hard-boiled eggs, chopped
1	cup chopped chives
1	cup crumbled cooked bacon
1	cup crumbled bleu cheese
¾	cup French dressing (see Index)
1¼	cups bleu cheese dressing (see Index)

MAUDE'S TABLE SIDE SALAD

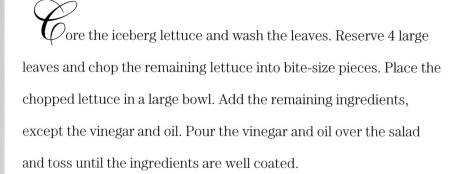

1 head iceberg lettuce

1 cup sliced hearts of palm

2 chopped hard-boiled eggs

¾ cup crumbled
    cooked bacon

¼ cup chopped chives

¾ cup crumbled bleu cheese

½ teaspoon
    Worcestershire sauce

½ teaspoon salt

½ teaspoon black pepper

¼ cup red wine vinegar

½ cup vegetable oil

Cherry tomatoes for garnish

Core the iceberg lettuce and wash the leaves. Reserve 4 large leaves and chop the remaining lettuce into bite-size pieces. Place the chopped lettuce in a large bowl. Add the remaining ingredients, except the vinegar and oil. Pour the vinegar and oil over the salad and toss until the ingredients are well coated.

Place lettuce leaves on four chilled plates. Mound salad in the center of each plate and garnish with cherry tomatoes.

REX SALAD

‰

*W*ash and core the lettuce. Reserve 4 large leaves for presentation; chop the remaining lettuce into bite-size pieces.

Place the chopped lettuce into a large bowl with the eggs, chives, bacon, bleu cheese, artichoke hearts, and hearts of palm. Toss the ingredients, then add the French and bleu cheese dressings. Toss the salad until well coated with dressing, then mound on chilled plates lined with lettuce leaves.

8 Servings

2	*heads iceberg lettuce*
4	*hard-boiled eggs, chopped*
1	*cup chopped chives*
1	*cup crumbled cooked bacon*
1	*cup crumbled bleu cheese*
2	*14-ounce cans artichoke hearts, drained and quartered*
1	*14-ounce can hearts of palm, drained and sliced*
¾	*cup French dressing (see Index)*
1¼	*cups bleu cheese dressing (see Index)*

SALMON SALAD ROYALE

6 Entrée Servings

---

1 tablespoon salt

¼ teaspoon black pepper

¼ teaspoon white pepper

½ teaspoon cayenne pepper

---

6 salmon fillets, about 6 to
8 ounces each

---

6 cups chopped
(1 large head)
romaine lettuce

---

24 strips of bacon,
fried crisp and
crumbled

1½ cups sliced hearts of palm

1½ cups warm vinaigrette
dressing (see Index)

---

3 cups croutons

---

6 ounces Chevre cheese,
crumbled

Preheat a grill or broiler.

*I*n a small bowl, combine the salt, black pepper, white pepper, and cayenne pepper. Sprinkle the salmon fillets on both sides with the seasoning mixture. Grill or broil the salmon until the meat is firm and flaky, about 4 to 7 minutes per side.

Place the salmon in a large bowl, and add the romaine, bacon, and hearts of palm. Toss the ingredients together, breaking the salmon into bite-size pieces.

Mound salad on 6 chilled plates, then spoon ¼ cup warm vinaigrette dressing over the greens. Top each salad with croutons and about 2 tablespoons crumbled Chevre cheese. If desired, garnish with fresh or pickled vegetables.

Seafood Salad James

In a large bowl, combine the vinegar, oil, Tabasco®, ketchup, and Worcestershire. Season to taste with salt and white pepper. Add the shrimp, crabmeat, celery, and chopped greens. Toss the ingredients until well coated with the dressing.

Place lettuce leaves on four chilled plates. Mound salad in the center of the leaves and garnish with tomato wedges and asparagus spears.

4 Entrée Servings

- *¼ cup red wine vinegar*
- *½ cup vegetable oil*
- *2 dashes of Tabasco®*
- *1 cup ketchup*
- *2 tablespoons Worcestershire sauce*
- *48 medium boiled shrimp, peeled and deveined (see Index)*
- *1 pound lump crabmeat, picked over to remove any shell and cartilage*
- *½ cup chopped celery*
- *2 cups chopped escarole*
- *2 cups chopped endive*
- *2 heads iceberg lettuce, cored and chopped*
- *4 large romaine lettuce leaves*
- *2 tomatoes, quartered*
- *8 blanched asparagus spears*
- *Salt and white pepper*

SHRIMP KATHLEEN

❧

8 Entrée Servings

1	small head iceberg lettuce
64	fresh asparagus spears, steamed or blanched
64	boiled shrimp, peeled and deveined (see Index)
3	cups Créole mayonnaise (see Index)

𝒞ore and wash the lettuce. Reserve 8 large leaves; shred the remaining lettuce.

Place lettuce leaves on eight chilled plates, then top with shredded lettuce. Arrange 8 asparagus spears and 8 shrimp on each plate. Spoon about ⅓ cup dressing over the salads and serve.

FRESH SPINACH SALAD

❧

4 Servings

10	ounces fresh spinach leaves, stemmed and washed
2	cups sliced mushrooms
8	strips of bacon, cooked and crumbled
1	cup Brennan dressing (see Index)
4	large lettuce leaves
8	thin slices onion
2	tablespoons chopped hard-boiled eggs

ℐn a large bowl, toss the spinach, mushrooms, bacon, and salad dressing. Line four chilled plates with lettuce leaves, then mound some of the dressed spinach on each leaf. Garnish the salads with onion slices and chopped egg.

TOMATOES LLORET

⁂

*P*lace the lettuce leaves on four chilled plates, then mound
½ cup shredded lettuce in the center of each leaf. Set a slice of
tomato on the shredded lettuce and top with crabmeat and onion.
Spoon 2 tablespoons of French dressing over the crabmeat and
garnish with chopped chives.

4 Servings

4	*large lettuce leaves*
2	*cups shredded lettuce*
4	*thin slices ripe tomato*
¼	*cup finely chopped onion*
12	*ounces lump crabmeat, picked over to remove any shell and cartilage*
½	*cup French dressing (see Index)*
½	*teaspoon chopped chives*

BLEU CHEESE DRESSING

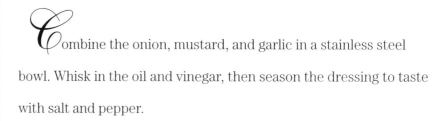

Yields 4 cups

---

1 cup Gorgonzola cheese

2 cups mayonnaise
(see Index)

1 cup heavy cream

1 cup sour cream

2 teaspoons lemon pepper
seasoning

Combine all of the ingredients in a medium bowl and mix thoroughly. Refrigerate the dressing for 2 hours before serving.

BRENNAN DRESSING

Yields 2½ cups

---

1 medium onion,
finely chopped

1 cup Créole mustard

2 tablespoons garlic,
finely chopped

¼ cup vegetable oil

½ cup red wine vinegar

Salt and black pepper

Combine the onion, mustard, and garlic in a stainless steel bowl. Whisk in the oil and vinegar, then season the dressing to taste with salt and pepper.

CAESAR DRESSING

Combine all of the ingredients, except the oil, in a stainless steel bowl. When the mixture is well blended, drizzle the oil into the bowl, whisking constantly, until all of the oil is incorporated. If the dressing seems too thick, cold water can be added, a little at a time, to adjust the consistency.

Yields 5 cups

2	ounces anchovies, (¼ cup) minced
4	egg yolks
2	teaspoons dry mustard
3	tablespoons lemon juice
3	tablespoons red wine vinegar
3	tablespoons horseradish
1	tablespoon minced garlic
1½	teaspoons black pepper
¼	cup freshly grated Romano cheese
¼	cup freshly grated Parmesan cheese
4	cups vegetable oil

FRENCH DRESSING

Beat the egg yolks in a stainless steel bowl until foamy and slightly thickened. Mix in the dry mustard. Add 1 cup of the oil, whisking constantly, then whisk in ¼ cup of the vinegar. Add the remaining oil and vinegar a third at a time, alternating the two ingredients. Stir in the Worcestershire and season to taste with salt and pepper. Refrigerate the dressing for 2 hours before serving.

Yields 5 cups

8	egg yolks
½	teaspoon dry mustard
3	cups vegetable oil
¾	cup red wine vinegar
½	teaspoon Worcestershire sauce

Salt and black pepper

CRÉOLE MAYONNAISE

Yields 1½ cups

---

2 tablespoons scallions,
    finely chopped

---

2 tablespoons parsley,
    finely chopped

½ teaspoon garlic,
    finely chopped

---

*Juice of 1 small lime
(Lemon can be substituted.)*

---

1 teaspoon Tabasco®

¼ cup Créole mustard

¾ cup mayonnaise
    (see Index)

---

2 egg whites

---

*I*n a stainless steel bowl, combine all of the ingredients, except the egg whites; blend thoroughly with a whisk.

In another bowl, whip the egg whites until thick. Using a whisk, gently fold the egg whites into the mayonnaise.Cover and chill the dressing before serving.

HOMEMADE MAYONNAISE

Yields 2¼ cups

---

2 egg yolks

½ teaspoon salt (or to taste)

---

1 teaspoon lemon juice

½ teaspoon dry mustard

Pinch of cayenne

---

2 cups vegetable oil

---

2 tablespoons boiling water

---

*C*ombine the egg yolks, salt, lemon juice, dry mustard, and cayenne in a mixing bowl; beat with an electric mixer or whisk until slightly thickened, about 5 minutes. Add 1 cup of the oil a teaspoon at a time, beating constantly, until the mixture becomes a thick emulsion. Add the remaining 1 cup of oil, 1 to 2 tablespoons at a time. When all of the oil is incorporated, beat in 2 tablespoons boiling water. Cover and refrigerate until use.

THOUSAND ISLAND DRESSING

*C*ombine all of the ingredients in a large mixing bowl, then cover and chill before serving.

2 cups ketchup

1 hard-boiled egg, chopped

½ cup pickle relish

1 cup mayonnaise
(see Index)

1 cup prepared chili sauce

1 tablespoon
Worcestershire sauce

¼ cup lemon juice

Salt and black pepper

VINAIGRETTE DRESSING

*I*n a large stainless steel bowl, combine the green bell pepper, red bell pepper, and scallions. Alternate the vinegar and oil, adding about ¼ cup vinegar at a time, followed by ½ cup salad oil. Blend in enough vinegar and oil to cover the chopped ingredients.

Fold the egg whites into the bell pepper mixture, then season with salt and pepper to taste. The vinaigrette is delicious cold or hot; chill it in the refrigerator or warm it slightly over low heat before serving.

1½ cups diced green
bell pepper

1½ cups diced red
bell pepper

1½ cups scallions,
finely chopped

½ cup red wine vinegar

1 cup vegetable oil

1½ cups chopped
hard-boiled egg whites

Salt and black pepper

BASIC OMELETTE

❧

2 Servings

4 large eggs

⅛ teaspoon salt

⅛ teaspoon black pepper

3 tablespoons butter

*I*n a small bowl, beat the eggs, salt, and pepper with a fork until blended. Melt the butter in an 8-inch skillet or omelette pan. Pour in the egg mixture and stir briskly. Cook the eggs over low heat; lift the edges of the omelette and shake the pan several times during cooking to keep the eggs from sticking. When the eggs are firm and the bottom is light brown, fold the omelette over and transfer it to a heated plate.

CAJUN ANDOUILLE OMELETTE WITH CHEDDAR CHEESE

❧

2 Servings

4 large eggs

⅛ teaspoon salt

⅛ teaspoon black pepper

3 tablespoons butter

¾ cup diced andouille or other spicy smoked sausage

¾ cup grated cheddar cheese

*I*n a small bowl, beat the eggs, salt, and pepper with a fork until blended. Melt the butter in an 8-inch skillet or omelette pan, then add the egg mixture and andouille, stirring briskly. Cook the eggs over low heat; lift the edges of the omelette and shake the pan several times during cooking to keep the eggs from sticking. When the eggs are almost set, fold in the cheese.Cook until the bottom forms a golden crust, then fold the omelette over and transfer it to a heated plate.

CHEDDAR AND HAM
OMELETTE

*I*n a small bowl, beat the eggs, salt, and pepper with a fork until blended. Melt the butter in an 8-inch skillet or omelette pan, then add the egg mixture and ham, stirring briskly. Cook the eggs over low heat; lift the edges of the omelette and shake the pan several times during cooking to keep the eggs from sticking. When the eggs are almost set, fold in the cheese. Cook until the bottom forms a golden crust, then fold the omelette over and transfer it to a heated plate.

2 Servings

4	eggs
1/8	teaspoon salt
1/8	teaspoon black pepper
3	tablespoons butter
3/4	cup diced ham
3/4	cup grated cheddar cheese

CRABMEAT OMELETTE

*I*n a small bowl, beat the eggs, salt, and pepper with a fork until blended. Melt the butter in an 8-inch skillet or omelette pan, then add the egg mixture and crabmeat, stirring briskly. Cook the eggs over low heat; lift the edges of the omelette and shake the pan several times during cooking to keep the eggs from sticking.

Cook until the bottom forms a golden crust, then fold the omelette over and transfer it to a heated plate. Top the omelette with hollandaise and serve.

2 Servings

4	large eggs
1/8	teaspoon salt
1/8	teaspoon black pepper
3	tablespoons butter
3/4	cup lump crabmeat, picked over to remove any shell or cartilage
1/2	cup hollandaise sauce (see Index)

CRAWFISH OMELETTE

2 Servings

4 large eggs
1/8 teaspoon salt
1/8 teaspoon black pepper
3 tablespoons butter
3/4 cup blanched crawfish
1/2 cup hollandaise sauce (see Index)

*I*n a small bowl, beat the eggs, salt, and pepper with a fork until blended. Melt the butter in an 8-inch skillet or omelette pan, then add the egg mixture and crawfish, stirring briskly. Cook the eggs over low heat; lift the edges of the omelette and shake the pan several times during cooking to keep the eggs from sticking.

Cook until the bottom forms a golden crust, then fold the omelette over and transfer it to a heated plate. Top the omelette with hollandaise and serve.

OMELETTE FLORENTINE

2 Servings

4 large eggs
1/8 teaspoon salt
1/8 teaspoon black pepper
3 tablespoons butter
3/4 cup stemmed and washed spinach leaves
3/4 cup creamed spinach (see Index)

*I*n a small bowl, beat the eggs, salt, and pepper with a fork until blended. Melt the butter in an 8-inch skillet or omelette pan, then add the egg mixture and spinach leaves, stirring briskly. Cook the eggs over low heat; lift the edges of the omelette and shake the pan several times during cooking to keep the eggs from sticking.

Cook until the bottom forms a golden crust, then fold the omelette over and transfer it to a heated plate. Top the omelette with creamed spinach and serve.

OMELETTE WITH FINE HERBS

⚜

*I*n a small bowl, beat the eggs, salt, and pepper with a fork until blended. Melt the butter in an 8-inch skillet or omelette pan, then add the egg mixture and fresh herbs, stirring briskly. Cook the eggs over low heat; lift the edges of the omelette and shake the pan several times during cooking to keep the eggs from sticking. Cook until the bottom forms a golden crust, then fold the omelette over and transfer it to a heated plate.

Note: Marjoram, thyme, basil, or any combination of fresh herbs can flavor the omelette.

2 Servings

4	large eggs
1/8	teaspoon salt
1/8	teaspoon black pepper
3	tablespoons butter
1	tablespoon scallions, finely chopped
1	tablespoon fresh oregano, finely chopped
1	tablespoon fresh parsley, finely chopped
1	tablespoon fresh chives, finely chopped

FRESH MUSHROOM OMELETTE

⚜

*I*n a small bowl, beat the eggs, salt, and pepper with a fork until blended. Melt the butter in an 8-inch skillet or omelette pan, then add the egg mixture and mushrooms, stirring briskly. Cook the eggs over low heat; lift the edges of the omelette and shake the pan several times during cooking to keep the eggs from sticking.

Cook until the bottom forms a golden crust, then fold the omelette over and transfer it to a heated plate. Top the omelette with brown sauce and serve.

2 Servings

4	large eggs
1/8	teaspoon salt
1/8	teaspoon black pepper
3	tablespoons butter
3/4	cup sliced mushrooms
1/2	cup brown sauce (see Index)

CAJUN TASSO OMELETTE WITH CHEDDAR CHEESE

≈

2 Servings

---

4 *large eggs*

⅛ *teaspoon salt*

⅛ *teaspoon black pepper*

3 *tablespoons butter*

¾ *cup diced tasso
(see note below)*

¾ *cup grated cheddar
cheese*

---

*I*n a small bowl, beat the eggs, salt, and pepper with a fork until blended. Melt the butter in an 8-inch skillet or omelette pan, then add the egg mixture and tasso, stirring briskly. Cook the eggs over low heat; lift the edges of the omelette and shake the pan several times during cooking to keep the eggs from sticking. When the eggs are almost set, fold in the cheese. Cook until the bottom forms a golden crust, then fold the omelette over and transfer it to a heated plate.

Note: Tasso is highly-seasoned Cajun smoked ham. If unavailable, substitute smoked ham and add cayenne pepper to taste.

POACHED EGGS

❦

*B*ring the water and vinegar to a boil in a large saucepan. Crack the eggs one at a time and drop them gently into the boiling water, being careful not to break the yolks. Simmer for 3 to 4 minutes, moving the eggs several times with a spoon to cook them evenly.

When firm, remove the eggs from the water with a slotted spoon and place in a pan filled with cold water until serving.

4 Servings

$1\frac{1}{2}$ quarts water
2 cups vinegar
8 large eggs

EGGS BENEDICT

❦

*M*elt the butter in a large sauté pan and warm the Canadian bacon over low heat. Place 2 Holland rusks on each plate and cover with slices of warm Canadian bacon. Set a poached egg on the bacon, then top each egg with hollandaise sauce. Serve immediately.

4 Servings

2 tablespoons butter
8 slices Canadian bacon (Smoked ham can be substituted.)
8 Holland rusks
8 poached eggs (see Index)
2 cups hollandaise sauce (see Index)

4 Servings

8 beef tournedos or filets
mignons, about
2 inches thick

¼ cup (½ stick) butter

8 Holland rusks (Halved
slices of toast can be
substituted.)

8 poached eggs (see Index)

1 cup pepper sauce
(see Index)

Salt and black pepper

Fresh chopped parsley
for garnish

4 Servings

4 beef filets, about
9 ounces each

Salt and black pepper

½ cup (1 stick) plus
2 tablespoons butter

8 slices Canadian bacon
(Smoked ham can be
substituted.)

8 Holland rusks

8 poached eggs (see Index)

2 cups hollandaise sauce
(see Index)

EGGS À LA CLARK

*S*eason the beef filets on both sides with salt and pepper. Melt the butter in a large sauté pan and cook the meat over medium heat for 2 to 3 minutes per side until medium rare.

Place 2 Holland rusks on each plate and top with the beef filets. Set a poached egg on the steaks, then spoon pepper sauce over the eggs. Sprinkle with chopped parsley and serve.

FILET OF BEEF BENEDICT

*S*eason the beef filets on both sides with salt and pepper. Melt ½ cup of the butter in a large sauté pan and cook the meat over medium heat for 5 to 6 minutes per side until medium rare.

While the filets are cooking, melt the remaining 2 tablespoons of butter in a large sauté pan and warm the Canadian bacon over low heat. Place 2 Holland rusks on each plate and cover with slices of warm Canadian bacon. Cut the beef filets in half and place one half on each Holland rusk. Set a poached egg on the steaks, then top each egg with hollandaise sauce. Serve immediately.

Note: A variation on this classic poached egg dish is Filet of Beef Hussarde. A generous spoonful of marchand de vin sauce napped between the beef filets and the poached eggs distinguishes Filet of Beef Hussarde from its single-sauced cousin.

EGGS ELLEN

Season the salmon with salt and pepper, then grill or broil the fish until flaky and cooked through, about 4 minutes per side.

Divide the salmon between four warm plates and top each fillet with a poached egg. Spoon hollandaise sauce over the eggs and serve.

4 Servings

8 *salmon fillets, about 3 ounces each*

8 *poached eggs (see Index)*

2 *cups hollandaise sauce (see Index)*

Salt and black pepper

Preheat a grill or broiler.

EGGS HUSSARDE

Melt the butter in a large sauté pan and warm the Canadian bacon over low heat.

Place 2 Holland rusks on each plate and cover with slices of warm Canadian bacon. Spoon marchand de vin sauce over the meat, then set a poached egg on each slice. Ladle hollandaise sauce over the eggs; garnish the plates with grilled tomatoes and serve.

4 Servings

2 *tablespoons butter*

8 *slices Canadian bacon (Ham can be substituted.)*

8 *Holland rusks*

2 *cups marchand de vin sauce (see Index)*

8 *poached eggs (see Index)*

2 *cups hollandaise sauce (see Index)*

Grilled tomatoes for garnish (see Index)

EGGS À LA NOUVELLE ORLÉANS

4 Servings

¼ cup (½ stick) plus
    1 tablespoon butter

¼ cup all-purpose flour

---

1 cup milk

---

2 cups heavy cream

---

1 tablespoon brandy

---

1 pound lump crabmeat,
    picked over to remove
    any shell and
    cartilage

---

8 poached eggs (see Index)

Salt and white pepper

Melt ¼ cup butter in a medium saucepan and stir in the flour. Cook the mixture for 5 minutes over medium heat, then gradually whisk in the milk and heavy cream. Reduce the heat and simmer the sauce for 10 minutes, stirring frequently, until thickened. Stir in the brandy and season with salt and pepper to taste.

In a medium sauté pan, melt the remaining tablespoon of butter, then add the crabmeat and cook for 1 to 2 minutes over medium heat.

Spoon ¼ cup hot crabmeat onto each plate and top with 2 poached eggs. Spoon cream sauce over the eggs and serve.

EGGS OWEN

*eel and cube the potato. Fill a large saucepan with water and bring the liquid to a boil. Add the potatoes to the boiling water and cook until tender, about 15 minutes; do not overcook.

Melt the butter in a large skillet and brown the beef tenderloin over moderately high heat, about 3 to 4 minutes. Remove the meat from the pan with a slotted spoon and set aside. Add the onions to the skillet and cook for 2 minutes, then stir in the celery, bell pepper, garlic, and bay leaves. Cook the vegetables for 2 to 3 minutes until tender, then blend in the Worcestershire, flour, scallions, cayenne, and white pepper. Season with salt and pepper to taste. Whisk the beef stock into the mixture and return the diced meat to the pan. When the mixture comes to a boil, lower the heat and simmer about 10 minutes, until the liquid has reduced. Remove the bay leaves and fold in the diced potatoes and parsley.

Spoon 2 portions of hash onto each serving plate, then place a poached egg on the hash. Ladle marchand de vin sauce over the eggs, garnish with grilled tomatoes and serve.

4 Servings

1	*large Idaho potato*
1/4	*cup (1/2 stick) butter*
1	*pound beef tenderloin, diced (Beef tips can be substituted.)*
1/2	*cup onion, finely chopped*
1/2	*cup celery, finely chopped*
1/2	*cup green bell pepper*
2	*tablespoons garlic, finely chopped*
2	*bay leaves*
1	*tablespoon Worcestershire sauce*
2	*tablespoons all-purpose flour*
1/2	*cup scallions, finely chopped*
	Pinch of cayenne pepper
	Pinch of white pepper
1	*cup beef stock (see Index)*
1/4	*cup fresh parsley, finely chopped*
	Salt and black pepper
8	*poached eggs (see Index)*
1/2	*cup marchand de vin sauce (see Index)*
	Grilled tomatoes for garnish (see Index)

EGGS PORTUGUESE

4 Servings

2 tablespoons olive oil

½ cup onion, finely chopped

½ cup celery, finely chopped

½ cup green bell pepper,
finely chopped

1½ tablespoons paprika

½ cup tomato juice

½ teaspoon Italian seasoning

1 bay leaf

1½ tablespoons tomato paste

1½ teaspoons garlic,
finely chopped

1½ cups fresh or canned
whole tomatoes

2 cups beef stock
(see Index)

1½ teaspoons cornstarch

1½ teaspoons
Worcestershire sauce

Salt and black pepper

8 medium patty shells

8 poached eggs (see Index)

2 cups hollandaise sauce
(see Index)

Heat the olive oil in a large saucepan or Dutch oven, then add the onion, celery, and bell pepper. Sauté the vegetables 2 to 3 minutes, then add the paprika and tomato juice. Reduce the heat and simmer for 10 minutes, stirring frequently. Add the Italian seasoning, bay leaf, tomato paste, garlic, and tomatoes, mashing the tomatoes with a fork. Pour in the stock and cook the mixture over moderately high heat for 15 minutes.

In a small bowl, blend together the cornstarch and 2 tablespoons water. Stir the liquid cornstarch into the sauce, then add the Worcestershire. Season with salt and pepper to taste and reduce the sauce until glossy and slightly thickened, 15 to 20 minutes. Remove the bay leaf before serving.

Place 2 warm patty shells on four heated plates. Spoon the Portuguese sauce into the patty shells, then place a poached egg in each. Ladle hollandaise sauce on top of the eggs and serve.

Eggs St. Charles

*I*n a shallow bowl, beat the egg with the milk. Season the trout with salt and pepper, then dredge the fillets in flour. Dip the fish in the egg wash and coat with corn flour.

Heat the oil or butter in a large skillet, then fry the fish over moderately high heat until crisp, about 4 to 5 minutes per side; blot on paper towels.

Divide the fried trout between four serving plates and top each fillet with a poached egg. Spoon hollandaise over the eggs and serve.

1 large egg

¼ cup milk

8 trout fillets, about 3 ounces each (Tilapia, drum or redfish can be substituted.)

½ cup all-purpose flour

½ cup corn flour

¼ cup vegetable oil or clarified butter

Salt and black pepper

8 poached eggs (see Index)

2 cups hollandaise sauce (see Index)

EGGS ST. DENIS

4 Servings

2	tablespoons butter
8	slices smoked ham, about ½-inch thick
8	Holland rusks (English muffins or buttered toast can be substituted.)
8	poached eggs (see Index)
3	cups marchand de vin sauce (see Index)

*M*elt the butter in a large skillet and warm the ham over low heat. Place 2 Holland rusks on each plate and top each with a slice of ham. Add 2 poached eggs. Spoon marchand de vin sauce over the eggs and serve.

EGGS SARDOU

4 Servings

8	artichokes
3	cups creamed spinach (see Index)
8	poached eggs (see Index)
2	cups hollandaise sauce (see Index)

*R*emove the stems of the artichokes and cut off the tops, removing all of the leaves. Steam or blanch the artichoke bottoms until tender, then scoop out the furry choke.

Mound creamed spinach on four plates and top with 2 warm artichoke bottoms. Set a poached egg in each artichoke bottom, spoon hollandaise sauce over the eggs and serve.

EGGS SHANNON

*In a shallow bowl, beat the egg with the milk. Season the trout with salt and pepper, then dredge the fillets in flour. Dip the fish in the egg wash and coat with corn flour.

Heat the oil or butter in a large skillet, then fry the fish over moderately high heat until crisp, about 4 to 5 minutes per side; blot on paper towels.

Make a bed of creamed spinach on four plates and top each with 2 fish fillets, followed by 2 poached eggs. Spoon hollandaise sauce over the eggs and serve.

4 Servings

1	large egg
¼	cup milk
8	trout fillets, about 3 ounces each (Tilapia, drum or redfish can be substituted.)
½	cup all-purpose flour
½	cup corn flour
¼	cup vegetable oil or clarified butter

Salt and black pepper

3	cups creamed spinach (see Index)
8	poached eggs (see Index)
2	cups hollandaise sauce (see Index)

HAM STEAK ROYALE

4 Servings

2	tablespoons butter
4	ham steaks, about ½-inch thick
8	poached eggs (see Index)
2	cups hollandaise sauce (see Index)

$\mathcal{M}$elt the butter in a large skillet and warm the ham steaks over low heat. Alternatively, the ham steaks can be grilled.

Transfer the ham steaks to heated plates and top with poached eggs. Spoon hollandaise sauce over the eggs and serve.

HAM STEAK BARBARIN

4 Servings

¼	cup (½ stick) butter
4	bananas, sliced lengthwise
¼	cup brown sugar
4	ham steaks, about ½-inch thick
4	teaspoons cracked black fresh peppercorns
½	teaspoon minced garlic
¼	cup honey

$\mathcal{M}$elt the butter in a large skillet and sauté the bananas about 1 minute on each side until tender. Transfer the bananas to heated plates and sprinkle with brown sugar. Press the cracked black peppercorns onto both sides of the ham steaks. Cook the ham steaks in the banana pan drippings until hot, but not dry. Add the garlic and honey to the pan and reduce for 1 minute. Set a ham steak in the center of each plate, flanked by the bananas. Spoon some of the honey glaze over the ham and serve.

GRILLED HAM STEAK
WITH EGGS THÉODORE

$\mathcal{M}$elt 2 tablespoons of the butter in a large skillet and warm the ham steaks over low heat. Transfer the ham steaks to a warm oven until serving.

Beat the eggs lightly with a pinch each of salt and pepper, then pour the mixture into a hot skillet containing 2 tablespoons melted butter. Cook over low heat, scrambling the eggs briskly with a fork until firm. Keep warm.

In a medium sauté pan, combine the brown sugar and remaining ½ cup of butter. Cook the mixture over low heat, stirring frequently, until the brown sugar dissolves and the ingredients are well blended; stir in the cinnamon and simmer another minute. Slice the bananas lengthwise and cook them in the cinnamon sauce until tender and heated through.

Set a ham steak in the center of each plate and spoon scrambled eggs on either side of the ham. Arrange 2 banana slices on the plate and pour some of the cinnamon sauce over the bananas. Serve immediately.

4 Servings

¾ cup (1½ sticks) butter

4 ham steaks, about ½-inch thick

8 large eggs

4 large bananas

½ cup brown sugar

1 tablespoon cinnamon

Salt and black pepper

GRILLADES AND GRITS

8 Servings

8	thinly pounded veal escalopes, about 3 ounces each
½	cup (1 stick) butter (Olive oil can be substituted.)
½	cup olive oil
½	cup chopped onion
½	cup chopped scallions
3	garlic cloves, finely chopped
1½	cups chopped green bell pepper
½	cup chopped celery
1	bay leaf
1½	teaspoons Italian seasoning
4	ripe tomatoes, diced
1	tablespoon Worcestershire sauce
2	tablespoons tomato paste
1	quart beef stock (see Index)
2	tablespoons cornstarch
¼	cup water
2	tablespoons chopped fresh parsley

Salt and black pepper

Plantation grits (see Index)

Preheat oven to 175 degrees F.

Season the veal escalopes on both sides with salt and pepper. Heat the butter in a large skillet and sauté the veal until lightly browned, about 3 minutes per side. Transfer the cooked meat to a platter and place in the warm oven while preparing the sauce.

Heat the olive oil in a large saucepan, then sauté the onions, scallions, garlic, bell pepper, and celery in the hot oil until tender. Stir in the bay leaf, Italian seasoning, tomatoes, Worcestershire, and tomato paste. When the mixture is well blended, add the beef stock and cook for 5 minutes, stirring frequently. In a small bowl, blend the cornstarch with ¼ cup water. Stir the liquid cornstarch into the sauce, then add the parsley. Season with salt and pepper to taste and cook over medium high heat until the sauce is reduced by about one fourth. Before serving, remove the bay leaf.

Spoon grillade sauce onto eight plates and center a veal escalope on each. Place cooked grits on the side of the meat, ladle additional sauce over the veal and grits, and serve.

Veal Shawn

Season the veal on both sides with salt and pepper, then dust with flour. Melt the butter in a large sauté pan and cook the escalopes over moderately high heat about 3 minutes per side.

Place the veal escalopes on serving plates, then top with poached eggs and hollandaise sauce.

8 Servings

---

8 veal escalopes, 4 to 6 ounces each, lightly pounded

All-purpose flour for dusting

½ cup (1 stick) butter

---

8 poached eggs (see Index)

---

2 cups hollandaise sauce (see Index)

Salt and black pepper

Veal Roussel

Season the veal with salt and pepper. Melt the butter in a large sauté pan and cook the escalopes over moderately high heat about 3 minutes per side; cook in batches if necessary.

Place 2 pieces of veal on eight ovenproof plates and top with 2 poached eggs. Cover each egg with a slice of Swiss cheese and place under a broiler to melt the cheese. Spoon grillade sauce over the dish and serve.

4 Servings

---

8 veal escalopes, 4 to 6 ounces each, lightly pounded

½ cup (1 stick) butter

---

8 poached eggs (see Index)

---

8 slices Swiss cheese

Grillade sauce (see Index)

Salt and black pepper

VEAL 417

✤

Season the veal on both sides with salt and pepper, then dust with flour. Melt the butter in a large sauté pan and cook the escalopes over moderately high heat about 3 minutes per side. Place the veal on serving plates and warm the crabmeat in the sauté pan. Top the veal with the crabmeat and hollandaise sauce, then garnish with chopped parsley.

Ingredients (left column)

4 Servings

4 veal escalopes, 4 to 6 ounces each, lightly pounded

All-purpose flour for dusting

¼ cup (½ stick) butter

12 ounces lump crabmeat, picked over to remove any shells and cartilage

1 cup hollandaise sauce (see Index)

Salt and black pepper

Chopped fresh parsley for garnish

CALVES' LIVER WITH SAUTÉED ONIONS

✤

Melt ½ cup of the butter in a large skillet and cook the onions over medium heat until lightly browned; transfer the onions to a platter and place in a warm oven.

In the same pan, melt the remaining ½ cup butter. Season the calves' liver on both sides with salt and pepper, then cook the slices over medium heat, about 8 to 10 minutes per side. Just before serving, place the onions on top of the liver and braise for 2 minutes.

Arrange slices of liver topped with sautéed onions on four dinner plates. Spoon warm grits onto the plates and serve.

Ingredients (Calves' Liver)

4 Servings

1 cup (2 sticks) butter

2 large onions, thinly sliced

2 pounds calves' liver, cut into 8 slices

Salt and black pepper

2 cups Plantation grits (see Index)

STEAK TARTARE ANASTASIA

*I*n a mixing bowl, whisk the egg yolks with 1 tablespoon of the paprika. Stir in the onion, capers, caper brine and dill relish. Chop the anchovies into a fine dice then, using the side of a chef's knife, smash the anchovies into a paste. Add the anchovy paste, along with the remaining ingredients (except the meat and garnish) to the caper mixture and whisk until well incorporated.

Place the ground sirloin in a glass or stainless steel bowl. Add half of the anchovy-caper mixture to the meat and mix thoroughly. Blend in the remaining tablespoon of paprika, then gradually stir in the rest of the anchovy-caper mixture. Mold the steak tartare on a platter lined with kale leaves; refrigerate for 1 to 2 hours. Garnish with toast rounds and serve.

4 Servings

3 egg yolks

2 tablespoons paprika

1 heaping tablespoon finely diced white onion

1 heaping tablespoon capers, finely chopped (reserve 2 tablespoons of the brine)

1 heaping tablespoon dill relish, finely chopped

3 anchovies

1 heaping tablespoon scallions, finely chopped

1 tablespoon chopped parsley

1 tablespoon Worcestershire sauce

2 tablespoons prepared steak sauce

1/4 teaspoon cayenne pepper

1 teaspoon ketchup

1 clove garlic, finely chopped

1 teaspoon red wine vinegar

1/8 teaspoon dry mustard

Salt to taste

1/4 teaspoon black pepper

1/4 teaspoon lemon juice

1 pound prime sirloin, heavily marbled, trimmed of fat and coarsely ground

Kale for garnish

Toast rounds or melba toast for garnish

SOFT SHELL CRAB CHÂRTRES

4 Servings

---
4 *large soft-shell crabs*
---
1 *egg*

¼ *cup milk*

All-purpose flour for dusting

Oil for deep frying

¼ *cup chopped capers*
---
1 *tablespoon chopped
fresh dill*
---
2 *cups hollandaise sauce
(see Index)*
---
2 *tablespoons butter*
---
8 *slices Canadian bacon*
---
8 *thick slices ripe tomato*

Salt and black pepper

Clean the crabs by removing the eyes and gills; trim the tails.

In a shallow bowl or pan, beat the egg with the milk. Season the crabs on both sides with salt and pepper, then dust lightly with flour. Dip the crabs in the egg wash and dust with flour again. Following the same procedure, batter the crabs in the flour and egg wash a second time. Deep fry the crabs in oil heated to 375 degrees F. Cook for 5 minutes until golden brown, then drain on paper towels.

Fold the capers and dill into the hollandaise and set aside.

Melt the butter in a large skillet and warm the Canadian bacon. Place 2 slices of Canadian bacon on each plate. Sauté the tomato slices in the skillet about 1 minute, then set the slices on the Canadian bacon. Top the tomato with the fried crab and cover with dill and caper sauce.

CRABMEAT IMPERIAL WITH HEARTS OF ARTICHOKE

❧

4 Servings

Preheat oven to 375 degrees F. In a large bowl, combine the crabmeat, scallions, bell pepper, pimento, egg yolk, dry mustard, artichoke hearts, paprika, and ½ cup of the mayonnaise. Stir until well mixed, then season with salt and pepper to taste.

Spoon the crabmeat mixture into four 1-cup baking dishes, then cover with the remaining mayonnaise. Sprinkle Parmesan and bread crumbs on top and bake in the hot oven for 15 to 20 minutes until heated through. Serve immediately.

Note: One pound of blanched crawfish tails can be substituted for the crabmeat.

Ingredients
1 pound lump crabmeat, picked over to remove any shell and cartilage (see note below)
½ cup scallions, finely chopped
½ cup green bell pepper, finely chopped
¼ cup chopped pimentos
1 egg yolk
1 teaspoon dry mustard
4 artichoke hearts, coarsely chopped
2 tablespoons paprika
1 cup mayonnaise (see Index)
¼ cup freshly grated Parmesan cheese
¼ cup seasoned bread crumbs
Salt and black pepper

STUFFED CRAB PARADIS

4 Servings

2½ cups seasoned
bread crumbs

½ cup oyster water or
fish stock (see Index)

½ cup (1 stick) butter

1 onion, finely chopped

½ cup shallots,
finely chopped

2 bay leaves

½ teaspoon salt

½ teaspoon black pepper

Pinch of cayenne pepper

8 ounces lump crabmeat,
picked over to remove
any shell and cartilage

1 tablespoon chopped
fresh parsley

*P*lace 2 cups bread crumbs in a bowl and dampen with the oyster water or fish stock.

Melt the butter in a large skillet and sauté the onion and shallots until tender. Add the dampened bread crumbs and cook for 3 to 5 minutes over medium heat. Fold in the bay leaves, salt, pepper, cayenne, crabmeat, and parsley; cook the mixture until heated through.

Preheat oven to 350 degrees F.

Remove the bay leaves and pack the stuffing into four well scrubbed crab shells or ramekins. Top with the remaining bread crumbs and place the shells on a baking sheet. Bake in the hot oven for 15 to 20 minutes. Serve the stuffed crabs with either Créole mayonnaise or lemon butter sauce (see the Index for recipes).

CRAB CAKES
WITH CRÉOLE MAYONNAISE

4 to 6 Servings

*C*ombine the ingredients, through the heavy cream, in a large bowl and stir until well mixed. Fold in the bread crumbs and season to taste with salt and pepper. Form the crab mixture by hand into 12 balls. Flatten the balls into cakes and place on wax or parchment paper.

Melt the butter in a large skillet and cook the crab cakes over medium heat until golden brown and heated through, about 6 minutes per side.

Serve immediately with Créole mayonnaise.

1	*pound lump crabmeat, picked over to remove any shell and cartilage (1 pound finely chopped blanched crawfish tails can be substituted.)*
¼	*cup celery, finely chopped*
¼	*cup green bell pepper, finely chopped*
¼	*cup scallions, finely chopped*
1	*teaspoon thyme leaves*
¼	*teaspoon cayenne pepper*
2	*large eggs, lightly beaten*
¼	*cup heavy cream*
¾	*cup seasoned bread crumbs*
2	*tablespoons butter*

Salt and black pepper

Créole mayonnaise (see Index)

CRAWFISH CHAMPAGNE

※

4 Servings

---

¹/₂ cup (1 stick) butter

---

1 pound blanched
   crawfish tails

---

¹/₂ cup diced shallots

---

1 cup champagne

---

2 cups heavy cream

---

4 medium puff
   pastry shells

---

*M*elt ¼ cup of the butter in a sauté pan and sauté the crawfish and shallots for 5 minutes. Add the champagne and reduce the amount of liquid by half, then pour in the cream. Lower the heat to medium and cook the sauce, stirring, until thickened. Fold in the remaining ¼ cup butter to finish the sauce.

Place a warm pastry shell on four plates and fill to overflowing with crawfish and sauce. Serve hot.

CRAWFISH ÉTOUFFÉE

$\mathcal{M}$elt ¾ cup butter in a large saucepan and sauté the onion and celery until tender. Add the garlic and cook another minute, then stir in the tomatoes, salt, pepper, crawfish, paprika, thyme, and bay leaves. Blend the flour into the mixture, then whisk in the chicken stock. Add the scallions, cayenne, and Worcestershire; cook over medium heat for 15 to 20 minutes, stirring occasionally. When the sauce has thickened, remove the bay leaves and fold in the parsley. Add the remaining 2 tablespoons butter to finish the sauce.

Serve the Crawfish Étouffée over hot rice and garnish with chopped parsley.

4 Servings

¾	cup (1½ sticks) plus 2 tablespoons butter
¾	cup onion, finely chopped
½	cup celery, finely chopped
1	tablespoon minced garlic
1	cup chopped fresh or canned tomatoes
¼	teaspoon salt (or to taste)
½	teaspoon black pepper
1	pound blanched crawfish tails
1	tablespoon paprika
1	teaspoon thyme leaves
2	bay leaves
3	tablespoons all-purpose flour
2	cups chicken stock (see Index)
¾	cup chopped scallions
Pinch of cayenne pepper	
1	tablespoon Worcestershire sauce
1	tablespoon chopped fresh parsley plus extra for garnish
2	cups white rice (see Index)

CRAWFISH SAMANTHA

4 Servings

½ cup (1 stick) butter

½ cup chopped
    white onion

---

1 cup sliced fresh
   mushrooms

¼ cup garlic, finely
   chopped

---

1 pound andouille or other
   spicy smoked sausage,
   sliced

---

2 pounds blanched
   crawfish tails (Peeled,
   deveined shrimp can
   be substituted.)

½ cup chopped scallions

---

1 tablespoon chopped
   parsley

½ cup white wine

---

2 cups white rice
   (see Index)

$\mathcal{M}$elt the butter in a large skillet and sauté the onion for several minutes until tender. Add the mushrooms and garlic, and cook the mixture for 3 to 4 minutes. Stir in the andouille, crawfish, and scallions, sauté an additional 4 minutes, then add the parsley and white wine. Reduce the heat and simmer briefly. Season with salt and pepper to taste.

Mound ½ cup rice on four plates and top with a generous serving of the crawfish mixture.

CRAWFISH SARDOU

In a shallow bowl or pan, lightly beat the eggs with the milk. Blend the flour, bread crumbs, black, white, and cayenne peppers in another bowl. Coat the crawfish with the dry mixture, then dip them in the egg wash. Redredge the crawfish in the dry mixture and deep fry them about 2 minutes until crisp, in oil heated to 350 degrees F.

Mound a bed of creamed spinach on four plates. Arrange a sliced artichoke bottom on the spinach, then divide the fried crawfish between the plates. Top the crawfish with about ½ cup of hollandaise and serve.

8 Servings

4	large eggs
1	cup milk
3	cups all-purpose flour
1½	cups seasoned bread crumbs
1½	teaspoons black pepper
1½	teaspoons white pepper
1½	teaspoons cayenne pepper
2	pounds blanched crawfish tails (Peeled and deveined shrimp can be substituted.)

Oil for deep frying

4	cups creamed spinach (see Index)
4	artichoke bottoms, thinly sliced
2	cups hollandaise sauce (see Index)

OYSTERS BENEDICT

4 Servings

3 cups corn flour
½ teaspoon salt
½ teaspoon black pepper
¼ teaspoon cayenne pepper
48 shucked oysters
Oil for deep frying
2 tablespoons butter
12 slices Canadian bacon (Smoked ham can be substituted.)
2 cups hollandaise sauce (see Index)
Grilled tomatoes for garnish (see Index)

*I*n a shallow bowl or pan, blend the corn flour with the salt, black pepper, and cayenne.

Dredge the oysters in the seasoned corn flour until well coated. Heat the oil in a deep fat fryer or large saucepan to 375 degrees F. Fry the oysters in the hot oil until golden brown, about 3 minutes. Drain on paper towels.

Melt the butter in a large skillet and warm the Canadian bacon; overlap 3 slices of Canadian bacon on each serving plate. Scatter a dozen fried oysters over the Canadian bacon and top with hollandaise. Garnish with grilled tomatoes and serve.

OYSTERS EN BROCHETTE

In a shallow bowl or pan, beat the eggs with the milk. Set the egg wash aside. Wrap the oysters in the bacon pieces and thread 12 oysters onto a skewer, spearing them through the bacon. Repeat the process, assembling four skewers in all. Season the wrapped oysters with salt and pepper, then dredge them in flour. Dip the skewers in egg wash, then recoat with flour.

Heat oil in a deep fryer or large saucepan to 375 degrees F.

Fry the oysters for 3 to 5 minutes until golden brown and crisp. Drain on paper towels.

Slide the oysters off the skewers onto four plates. Top the Oysters en Brochette with lemon butter sauce and serve brabant potatoes on the side.

4 Servings

2	*large eggs*
½	*cup milk*
48	*shucked oysters*
12	*strips of bacon, quartered*

All-purpose flour for dredging

Salt and black pepper

Oil for deep frying

1½ *cups lemon butter sauce (see Index)*

Brabant potatoes (see Index)

ENTRÉES   155

CHEF MIKE'S OYSTER LOAF

4 Servings

---

3 *cups corn flour*

½ *teaspoon cayenne pepper*
(or to taste)

---

48 *shucked oysters*

Vegetable oil for deep frying

---

2 *large loaves French*
bread

---

2 *tablespoons minced*
garlic

¼ *cup (½ stick) butter*

---

4 *tablespoons mayonnaise*
(see Index)

---

1 *cup shredded lettuce*

---

2 *medium tomatoes, sliced*

---

1 to 2 lemons, seeded and
finely sliced

---

1 *sliced dill pickle*

Salt and freshly ground
black pepper

Tabasco®

Place the corn flour in a shallow bowl or pan and season with cayenne pepper, salt, and black pepper.

Drain the oysters thoroughly, then roll them in the seasoned corn flour. In a deep fat fryer or large pot, heat vegetable oil to 375 degrees F. Fry the oysters in batches about 3 minutes until crisp and golden brown. Drain on paper towels and keep warm.

Preheat oven to 400 degrees F.

Slice the loaves of bread in half, then split them open horizontally. Spread ½ tablespoon minced garlic and a tablespoon each of butter and mayonnaise on the inner sides of the loaves. On the bottom halves of the loaves, divide the lettuce, fried oysters, tomato, dill pickle, and lemon slices. Sprinkle with a few drops Tabasco®.

Cover the sandwiches with their bread tops, transfer to a baking sheet, then bake briefly in a hot oven until the bread is crisp, 3 to 5 minutes. Serve immediately.

OYSTERS PAN ROAST WARREN

4 Servings

Melt the butter in a large skillet and sauté the shallots for 2 to 3 minutes until tender. Blend in the flour and cook over medium heat for 3 to 5 minutes, stirring, then whisk in the oyster water and cayenne. When the sauce begins to thicken, fold in the oysters and cook until heated through.

Preheat a broiler.

Pour the mixture into four 1-cup baking dishes and sprinkle Parmesan over the top, then broil about 2 minutes until the cheese begins to brown. Serve with toast points.

1	cup (2 sticks) butter
⅔	cup chopped shallots
½	cup all-purpose flour
2	cups oyster water (If necessary, add water to yield this volume.)
¼	teaspoon cayenne pepper
24	shucked oysters
2	tablespoons freshly grated Parmesan cheese
4	slices of toasted bread for garnish

STUFFED SHRIMP COCODRIE

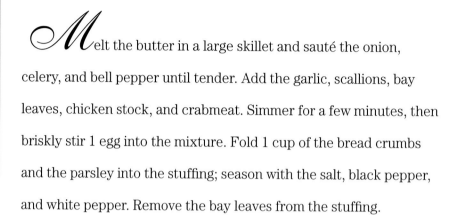

4 Servings

½	cup (1 stick) butter
1	medium onion, finely chopped
¾	cup chopped celery
1	cup chopped green bell pepper
2	garlic cloves, minced
½	cup scallions, finely chopped
2	bay leaves
1	cup chicken stock (see Index)
8	ounces lump crabmeat, picked over to remove any shell and cartilage
3	large eggs
2½	cups seasoned bread crumbs
1	tablespoon chopped fresh parsley
½	teaspoon salt
½	teaspoon black pepper
½	teaspoon white pepper
16	large shrimp, peeled, deveined and butterflied
½	cup milk
All-purpose flour for dredging	
Oil for deep frying	

Melt the butter in a large skillet and sauté the onion, celery, and bell pepper until tender. Add the garlic, scallions, bay leaves, chicken stock, and crabmeat. Simmer for a few minutes, then briskly stir 1 egg into the mixture. Fold 1 cup of the bread crumbs and the parsley into the stuffing; season with the salt, black pepper, and white pepper. Remove the bay leaves from the stuffing.

In a shallow bowl or pan, beat the remaining 2 eggs with the milk. Pack stuffing onto each shrimp and dredge in flour. Roll the stuffed shrimp in the egg wash and coat with the remaining 1½ cups bread crumbs.

Deep fry the breaded shrimp in oil heated to 350 degrees F. Fry about 6 minutes until golden brown, drain and serve.

SHRIMP CRÉOLE

Melt the butter in a large saucepan and cook the bell pepper, onion, celery, and garlic until tender, 5 to 8 minutes. Stir in the tomato paste, paprika, and Italian seasoning and cook an additional 3 minutes. Add 1½ cups chicken stock or water, tomato juice, tomatoes, Worcestershire, salt, black, cayenne, and white peppers. Bring the mixture to a boil, then reduce the heat and simmer for 8 to 10 minutes, stirring frequently.

In a small bowl, blend the cornstarch with 4 tablespoons water until smooth. Gradually add the cornstarch to the shrimp sauce, stirring constantly, until the sauce thickens. Add the shrimp and parsley to the sauce and bring the mixture to a boil. Lower the heat and simmer for 5 to 8 minutes until the shrimp are cooked through; do not overcook.

Serve the Shrimp Créole over cooked rice.

Note: Pasta can be substitued for rice.

½ cup (1 stick) butter

1½ cups chopped green bell pepper

1½ cups chopped onion

1½ cups chopped celery

1 tablespoon garlic, finely chopped

¼ cup tomato paste

2 tablespoons paprika

1½ teaspoons Italian seasoning

1½ cups chicken stock or water

1 cup tomato juice

1 cup peeled and chopped tomatoes

1½ teaspoons Worcestershire sauce

1½ teaspoons salt

Pinch of black pepper

Pinch of cayenne pepper

Pinch of white pepper

1½ tablespoons cornstarch

4 tablespoons water

3 pounds medium shrimp, peeled and deveined

¼ cup chopped fresh parsley

4 cups white rice (see Index)

SHRIMP AND PASTA BORDELAISE

6 to 8 Servings

1 pound angel hair pasta
1 cup (2 sticks) butter
5 chopped shallots
3 tablespoons chopped garlic
2 pounds peeled and deveined medium shrimp (see note below)
½ cup dry white wine
1 teaspoon white pepper
1 bunch chopped scallions
3 tablespoons chopped fresh parsley

Boil the pasta in boiling water according to the package directions and drain. Melt ½ cup of the butter in a large sauté pan and sauté the shallots for 30 seconds. Add the garlic, cook another 30 seconds, then stir in the shrimp. Cook over moderately high heat until the tails of the shrimp curl, then reduce the heat to medium and add the wine. Cook the mixture for 5 minutes, then add the pepper, scallions, and parsley. Lower the heat and simmer the sauce for a few minutes.

Just before serving, toss the drained pasta in the sauce, then remove the pan from the heat and fold in the remaining ½ cup of butter.

Note: Two pounds of blanched crawfish tails can be substituted for the shrimp.

SHRIMP VICTORIA

Melt the butter in a large saucepan and sauté the shrimp for 1 minute. Add the mushrooms and sauté another minute, then stir in the basil and flour. Cook the mixture for 2 to 3 minutes, stirring, then pour in the hot milk and cream. When well blended, add the scallions, salt, pepper, and wine. Reduce the sauce until thickened, stirring frequently.

Just before serving, fold in the parsley and sour cream; cook a few minutes over very low heat to warm the sauce.

Serve Shrimp Victoria over white rice.

6 to 8 Servings

¼ cup (½ stick) butter
2 pounds peeled and deveined medium shrimp
3 cups sliced mushrooms
1 teaspoon basil leaves
½ cup all-purpose flour
2 cups hot milk
2 cups heavy cream
1 cup chopped scallions
½ teaspoon salt
¼ teaspoon white pepper
¼ cup dry white wine
1 tablespoon chopped fresh parsley
½ cup sour cream

SALMON CRAWFISH ROBERT

½ cup (1 stick) butter

¼ cup shallots, finely
chopped

½ cup chopped scallions

---

1 cup sliced mushrooms

---

1 pound blanched
crawfish tails

---

1 cup champagne

---

1 cup heavy cream

---

4 salmon fillets, about
5 ounces each

All-purpose flour for dredging

Salt and white pepper

---

*M*elt ¼ cup of the butter in a large sauté pan and cook the
shallots, scallions, and mushrooms over medium heat about
5 minutes until tender. Stir in the crawfish and cook until the
crawfish tails curl tightly. Pour in the champagne and bring the
mixture to a gentle boil. Add the cream and season with salt and
white pepper to taste. Reduce over medium heat until thick enough
to coat a spoon. Remove the pan from the heat and finish the sauce
with 2 tablespoons butter.

Season the salmon on both sides with salt and pepper, then dredge
in flour. Melt the remaining 2 tablespoons butter in a large skillet and
cook the salmon about 6 to 8 minutes per side until the fish is flaky
but not dry.

Transfer the salmon fillets to four plates, top with crawfish sauce
and serve.

GRILLED SALMON STEAK AUDUBON

Sprinkle the salmon on both sides with salt and pepper.

Grill or broil the fillets until firm and flaky, about 6 minutes per side.

Set the salmon aside.

Blanch the grated carrot in boiling water for 1 minute, then remove

with a slotted spoon and drain on a clean cloth.

In a medium bowl, combine the hollandaise and Créole mustard.

Stir well, then fold the carrot and shrimp into the sauce.

Spoon sauce over the salmon and broil 1 to 2 minutes

to glaze the fish. Serve immediately.

4 Servings

4	salmon fillets, about 6 ounces each
1	large carrot, grated
2	cups hollandaise sauce (see Index)
½	cup Créole mustard
8	ounces boiled small shrimp, peeled and deveined (see Index)

Salt and black pepper

Preheat a grill or broiler to 375 – 400 degrees F.

GRILLED SALMON PACIFICA

4 Servings

4 *salmon fillets, 4 to 6
   ounces each*

3 *tablespoons chopped
   fresh dill*

4 *tablespoons capers, finely
   chopped*

2 *cups hollandaise sauce
   (see Index)*

Salt and black pepper

*Steamed or sautéed mixed
   fresh vegetables for
   garnish*

*Preheat a grill or broiler
to 375 – 400 degrees F.*

*S*eason the salmon fillets on both sides with salt and pepper.
Grill or broil the salmon until flaky and cooked through, about
6 minutes per side. Transfer the salmon to heated serving plates.

Fold the dill and capers into the hollandaise sauce, then spoon
about a half cup of the mixture over the salmon fillets. Garnish
the plates with cooked fresh vegetables and serve.

FILLET OF DOVER SOLE ARIAN

Heat the cream in a large sauté pan over medium heat to just below the boiling point.

Butter four 12 x 12-inch sheets of aluminum foil and place 8 ounces of Dover sole in the center of each. On each square, layer the fish fillet with a dill sprig, one quarter of the lobster medallions, and 2 tablespoons crabmeat. Fold the foil over the ingredients and wrap tightly. Poach the packets in the hot cream for 15 minutes, turning once or twice during cooking.

While the fish is poaching, sauté the apple rings until tender in 2 tablespoons butter. Keep warm until serving.

Remove the foil from the fish packets and drain the excess poaching liquid. Arrange 3 or 4 apple slices on four plates and top with the Dover sole and seafood. Spoon lemon butter sauce over the dish and serve.

4 Servings

1	quart heavy cream
2	tablespoons butter plus extra for buttering aluminum foil
32	ounces Dover sole fillets
4	fresh dill sprigs
2	cooked lobster tails, shelled and sliced into medallions
4	ounces lump crabmeat, picked over to remove any shell and cartilage
1	large apple, cored and sliced into thin rings
1	cup lemon butter sauce (see Index)

STUFFED FLOUNDER MANCHAC

4 Servings

6	tablespoons butter
1	cup onion, finely chopped
1	cup scallions, finely chopped
½	cup green bell pepper, finely chopped
4	garlic cloves, minced
¼	cup all-purpose flour
2	teaspoons paprika
½	cup dry white wine
2	cups fish stock (see Index)

Pinch of cayenne pepper

2	egg yolks, lightly beaten
¾	cup seasoned bread crumbs
¼	cup fresh parsley, finely chopped
8	ounces lump crabmeat, picked over to remove any shell and cartilage
8	ounces medium shrimp, peeled and deveined
24	shucked oysters
4	whole flounders, about 1½ pounds each
¼	cup freshly grated Parmesan cheese
¼	cup vegetable oil

Salt and black pepper

Melt the butter in a large skillet and sauté the onion, scallions, bell pepper, and garlic until tender. Blend in the flour and cook the mixture over medium heat about 4 minutes, stirring constantly; do not brown the flour. Add the paprika, wine, and fish stock. Stir until the mixture is smooth, then season with cayenne, salt, and pepper. Add the egg yolks and stir briskly, then fold in ½ cup of the bread crumbs and the parsley. Add the crabmeat, shrimp, and oysters, and cook over low heat about 5 minutes until the mixture is heated through. Remove the stuffing from the heat and keep warm while preparing the flounder.

Preheat oven to 375 degrees F.

Remove the head from each flounder and lay the fish on their sides with the dark side facing up. Using a sharp knife, make a slit down the center of the fish, from the head end to the tail. Bone the fish through the slit and fill the resulting cavity with the stuffing.

Combine the remaining ¼ cup bread crumbs with the Parmesan cheese and sprinkle the mixture over the stuffing. Close the fish and brush the outside with vegetable oil. Place the fish on oiled baking sheets and bake in the hot oven for 30 minutes. Serve immediately.

LOBSTER 417

$\mathcal{B}$ring 6 quarts of salted water to a boil in a large, deep pot. Add the lobsters and cook for 6 to 8 minutes. Drain the lobsters and set them aside to cool. When cool enough to handle, split the lobsters in half lengthwise, then remove and discard the head sacs. Extract and chop the tail meat; set the meat aside while preparing the sauce. Reserve the lobster shells.

Melt the butter in a large skillet, then sauté the scallions and mushrooms for several minutes until tender. Stir in the flour and cook the mixture over low heat for 3 to 5 minutes. Add the chopped lobster and cream; stir until smooth, then season with salt, pepper, and cayenne. Working quickly, stir the egg yolks into the hot mixture. When the yolks are hot, add the parsley and sherry.

Place a split lobster shell on each plate and fill both halves with the meat and sauce. Garnish the lobsters with chopped parsley and serve.

4 Servings

---

4 *spiny lobsters, about*
   1½ pounds each

---

6 *quarts salted water*

½ *cup (1 stick) butter*

---

1 *cup chopped scallions*

---

1 *cup sliced mushrooms*

¼ *cup all-purpose flour*

---

3 *cups heavy cream*

¼ *to ½ teaspoon cayenne*

---

4 *egg yolks, lightly beaten*

---

2 *tablespoons chopped*
   fresh parsley, plus
   extra for garnish

½ *cup sherry*

Salt and black pepper

POMPANO EN PAPILLOTE

4 Servings

24	shucked oysters
1	cup dry white wine
½	cup (1 stick) butter
1	cup scallions, finely chopped
1	teaspoon minced garlic
1	cup quartered mushrooms
1	tablespoon all-purpose flour
2	cups (12 ounces) cooked peeled shrimp
2	egg yolks

Pinch of cayenne

4	pompano fillets, about 6 ounces each

Salt and black pepper

Parchment Paper;
  4 18-inch squares

*B*lanch the oysters in their water with half of the wine; cook just until the edges of the oysters curl. Set the oysters and oyster stock aside.

Melt ¼ cup butter in a large skillet and cook the scallions, garlic, and mushrooms over medium heat. Blend in the flour and cook about 3 minutes, stirring constantly; do not let the flour brown. Reduce the heat to low and add the remaining wine, oysters, oyster stock, and shrimp. Simmer the mixture until the liquid has reduced by half, then remove the pan from the heat; working quickly, stir in the egg yolks. Season the mixture with the cayenne and salt and pepper.

Place the pompano in another large skillet and add water almost to cover. Season with salt and bring the water to a boil. Lower the heat, then simmer about 5 minutes. Drain the poached fillets on paper towels and set aside.

Preheat oven to 375 degrees F.

Fold an 18-inch square of parchment paper in half, then trim it into the shape of one half of a heart, making a whole heart when unfolded. Repeat, making four parchment paper hearts in all.

Brush the paper hearts with the remaining ¼ cup butter, then spoon some of the shrimp mixture on one side of the paper. Set a pompano fillet on top of the shrimp, then spoon more of the shrimp mixture over the fillet. Close the parchment paper and fold the edges together to seal the cases. Transfer the cases to baking sheets and bake in the hot oven for 10 to 15 minutes until the paper balloons and turns golden brown. Serve immediately.

POMPANO GRAND DUC

4 Servings

5 tablespoons butter

¼ cup scallions, finely chopped

¼ cup all-purpose flour

2¾ cups fish stock (see Index)

3 tablespoons dry white wine

¼ teaspoon salt

Pinch of cayenne pepper

1 egg yolk, lightly beaten

4 pompano fillets, about 6 ounces each

½ cup heavy cream

½ cup hollandaise sauce (see Index)

2 cups seasoned mashed potatoes (see Index)

6 asparagus spears, steamed or blanched until tender

24 boiled shrimp, peeled and deveined (see Index)

24 blanched oysters

Preheat oven to 375 degrees F.

*M*elt 3 tablespoons of the butter in a large skillet and sauté the scallions a few minutes until tender. Blend in the flour and reduce the heat to low. Cook the mixture 5 minutes, stirring constantly; do not brown the flour. Whisk in ¾ cup of the fish stock, the wine, salt, and cayenne. When the mixture is smooth, add the egg and stir briskly. Simmer over low heat, stirring constantly, for 15 minutes. Remove the fish sauce from the heat and keep warm until serving.

Combine the remaining 2 tablespoons butter and 2 cups fish stock in a large sauté pan. Heat the liquid until just below the boiling point, then place the pompano in the pan and poach about 5 minutes until flaky and cooked through, turning the fillets once. Remove the fish from the pan and drain on a clean cloth.

Place the heavy cream in a small bowl and whip until stiff, then fold in the hollandaise sauce.

Fill a pastry bag with the mashed potatoes and pipe potatoes around the edge of a large, warm platter. Place the asparagus spears in the center of the platter and cover with the warm fish sauce. Arrange the pompano fillets on the fish sauce and garnish with the shrimp and oysters. Pour the hollandaise and cream mixture over the seafood and bake in the hot oven for 3 to 4 minutes until the potatoes begin to brown. Serve immediately.

Brennan's Blackened Redfish

6 Servings

$\mathcal{I}$n a small bowl, combine the cayenne, black pepper, white pepper, and salt. Set the seasoning mixture aside. Place the redfish in a shallow dish and pour the Worcestershire sauce over the fillets. Marinate the fish for 30 minutes in the refrigerator, turning the fish several times.

Sprinkle the marinated fillets on both sides with the seasoning mixture. Coat a large cast iron skillet with the oil and heat until almost smoking. Place the redfish in the hot skillet and sear about 2 minutes per side, until the seasoning mixture has melted into the fish.

Serve the redfish plain or top with lemon butter sauce.

1	tablespoon cayenne pepper
1	tablespoon black pepper
1	tablespoon white pepper
½	teaspoon salt (or less to taste)
6	redfish fillets, 6 to 8 ounces each (Tilapia, drum or trout can be substituted.)
1	cup Worcestershire sauce
1	tablespoon vegetable oil
1½	cups lemon butter sauce (see Index)

REDFISH DUNCAN

4 Servings

---

3 tablespoons butter

---

1 cup chopped pecans

---

2 teaspoons Worcestershire
   sauce

Pinch of salt

Pinch of garlic powder

Pinch of cayenne

Pinch of dry mustard

Pinch of thyme leaves

Pinch of crushed bay leaf

---

4 redfish fillets, about 8
   ounces each
   (Tilapia, drum or trout
   can be substituted.)

---

1 cup champagne

---

3 cups water

---

1 pound lump crabmeat,
   picked over to remove
   any shell and cartilage

½ cup lemon butter sauce
   (see Index)

Melt 2 tablespoons of the butter in a small skillet, then add the pecans and Worcestershire. Cook the pecans over medium heat for 30 seconds and set aside.

In a small bowl, combine the salt, garlic powder, cayenne, dry mustard, thyme, and bay leaf. Sprinkle the redfish on one side with the seasoning mixture, then place the fillets in a large sauté pan. To the pan, add the champagne and 3 cups of water. Cover the fish with a clean towel and poach over medium heat for 10 minutes.

In another small skillet, melt the remaining 1 tablespoon butter and warm the crabmeat gently over low heat.

Remove the cooked fish from the pan, blot dry, then place on four plates. Divide the crabmeat between the fillets and top with the sautéed pecans. Spoon lemon butter sauce over the redfish and serve.

REDFISH GELPI

*M*elt the butter in a large skillet and sauté the shallots, bell pepper, and garlic until tender. Add the pimento, capers, vinegar, Worcestershire, salt, cayenne, and fish stock. Simmer the mixture for 10 minutes, then stir in the parsley. Remove the sauce from the heat and keep warm while preparing the fish.

Preheat a broiler.

Season the redfish fillets on both sides with salt and pepper. Broil the fish until flaky and cooked through.

Place the redfish fillets on serving plates, cover with sauce and serve.

4 Servings

½	cup (1 stick) butter
¾	cup shallots, finely chopped
¼	cup chopped green bell pepper
1	teaspoon minced garlic
¼	cup chopped pimento
1	tablespoon capers, rinsed
1	teaspoon tarragon vinegar
1	teaspoon Worcestershire sauce
1	teaspoon salt
¼	teaspoon cayenne pepper
½	cup fish stock (see Index)
1	tablespoon chopped parsley
4	redfish fillets, 6 to 8 ounces each (Tilapia, drum or trout can can be substituted.)

REDFISH COLLIER

4 Servings

---

4 redfish fillets, 4 to 6
   ounces each (Tilapia,
   trout or drum can be
   substituted.)

All-purpose flour for dusting

---

1 cup (2 sticks) butter

---

8 ounces mushrooms,
   cleaned

---

2 tablespoons chopped
   onion

---

32 ounces fresh spinach,
   stemmed and chopped

¼ cup dry white wine

Pinch of nutmeg

---

1 cup warm lemon butter
   sauce (see Index)

---

4 teaspoons crumbled
   cooked bacon

---

4 teaspoons scallions,
   finely chopped

---

1 teaspoon chopped fresh
   parsley

---

8 slices Swiss cheese

---

*L*ightly dust the redfish with flour. Melt ½ cup butter in a large skillet, add the fillets and mushrooms, then sauté until the fish is fully cooked, about 2½ minutes per side. Transfer the fillets and mushrooms to a platter and keep warm.

Drain the skillet and add the remaining ½ cup of butter. Sauté the onions in the butter for several minutes until tender, then add the spinach and wine. Season with the nutmeg, salt, and pepper; cook over medium heat several minutes until the spinach is wilted.

In a small bowl, combine the lemon butter, bacon, scallions, and parsley. Blend the ingredients together and let stand at room temperature.

To serve, place the redfish fillets on ovenproof plates. Top the fish with the cooked spinach, then arrange several mushroom caps on top of the spinach. Place slices of Swiss cheese over the mushrooms, then broil briefly until the cheese melts. Spoon sauce on the side of the fish and serve.

REDFISH JAMIE

Melt 2 tablespoons of the butter in a large saucepan over medium heat and add the garlic, mushrooms, paprika, and tomato paste. Cook the mixture for 2 to 3 minutes, stirring constantly, then blend in 2 tablespoons flour. Add the scallions, Worcestershire, and chicken stock and whisk the mixture with a wire whisk. Season with salt and pepper, then stir in the parsley and wine. Simmer the sauce for 15 to 20 minutes, stirring frequently.

While the sauce is cooking, prepare the redfish. Sprinkle the fillets on both sides with salt and pepper, then dredge in flour.

Melt ¼ cup butter in a large skillet and cook the fish over moderately high heat about 5 minutes until flaky; turn the fillets once during cooking.

Carefully fold the crabmeat into the sauce.

Transfer the fillets to warm plates and top with sauce.

4 Servings

¼ cup (½ stick) plus 2 tablespoons butter

1½ teaspoons minced garlic

2 cups sliced mushrooms

2 teaspoons paprika

¼ cup tomato paste

2 tablespoons all-purpose flour plus extra for dredging

1 cup sliced scallions

1½ teaspoons Worcestershire sauce

1½ cups chicken stock (see Index)

2 teaspoons chopped fresh parsley

¼ cup Burgundy wine

4 redfish fillets, 3 to 4 ounces each (Tilapia, drum or trout can be substituted.)

1 pound lump crabmeat, picked over to remove any shell and cartilage

Salt and white pepper

FILLET OF REDFISH MICHAEL

4 Servings

---

4 redfish fillets, 4 to 6
    ounces each (Tilapia,
    drum or trout can be
    substituted.)

All-purpose flour for dredging

½ cup (1 stick) butter

---

1 large carrot, peeled and
   julienned

---

1 zucchini, julienned

Salt and black pepper

---

2 cups Brennan's red wine
   mushroom sauce
   (see Index)

---

*S*eason the redfish fillets on both sides with salt and pepper, then dredge them in flour. Melt ¼ cup butter in a large skillet, then sauté the fillets until fully cooked, about 4 to 6 minutes per side. Keep the redfish warm until serving.

In another skillet, melt the remaining ¼ cup butter and stir fry the carrots and zucchini for 7 minutes over high heat; the vegetables should still be crunchy.

Mound a bed of carrots and zucchini on four serving plates. Place a redfish fillet on top of the vegetables, then spoon about ½ cup red wine mushroom sauce over the fish.

REDFISH PEREZ

Season the redfish on both sides with salt and pepper, then dredge in flour. Melt the butter in a large skillet and sauté the redfish for 4 to 5 minutes per side. Transfer the fish to a warm platter and add the shrimp and crabmeat to the pan. Cook over medium heat until the shrimp turn pink and are cooked through, about 5 minutes.

To serve, top the redfish with the shrimp and crabmeat, then cover with hollandaise sauce.

---

4 *redfish fillets, 6 to 8 ounces each (Tilapia, drum or trout can be substituted.)*

All-purpose flour for dredging

½ *cup (1 stick) butter*

---

12 *large shrimp, peeled and deveined*

---

12 *ounces lump crabmeat, picked over to remove any shell and cartilage*

Salt and black pepper

---

2 *cups hollandaise sauce (see Index)*

REDFISH AU POIVRE CAJUN

᯽

4 Servings

---

2 teaspoons cracked
   peppercorns

---

4 redfish fillets, about
   6 ounces each
   (Tilapia, drum or trout
   can be substituted.)

All-purpose flour for dusting

---

3 tablespoons butter

---

1 cup pepper sauce
   (see Index)

*P*ress about ¼ teaspoon cracked peppercorns onto each side of
the four redfish fillets, then dust them lightly with flour. Melt
the butter in a heavy sauté pan. Sauté the redfish in the butter for
4 to 5 minutes per side; transfer the cooked fillets to heated plates.
Spoon pepper sauce over the fish and garnish with steamed
fresh vegetables.

COLD POACHED REDFISH
WITH STUFFED PEPPERS

᯽

4 Servings

---

2 teaspoons salt (or less
   to taste)

2½ teaspoons paprika

1½ teaspoons lemon pepper

---

2 teaspoons onion powder

---

2 teaspoons oregano

---

1 teaspoon mustard seeds

½ teaspoon sesame seeds

½ teaspoon cayenne pepper

*I*n a small bowl, blend the ingredients, through the cayenne
pepper. Fill a large saucepan with water and add the seasoning
mixture. Boil the water for 15 minutes, then strain through a fine
sieve into another saucepan. Return the strained stock to a boil
and poach the redfish fillets until firm, about 5 minutes. Blot on
paper towels.

Blanch the spinach leaves in the stock about 30 seconds until wilted,
then drain on paper towels. Blanch and drain the lettuce leaves.
Reserve the stock.

Spread four sheets of plastic wrap on a work surface and place a poached fillet in the center of each. Wrap the fillets with 3 spinach leaves, then with 3 lettuce leaves. Grill the shrimp and arrange 6 cooked shrimp on top of each wrapped fillet. Fold the plastic wrap over the fish bundles, sealing them tightly; refrigerate for 2 to 3 hours.

Bring the stock back to a boil and drop the quartered red and yellow bell peppers into the stock. Boil the peppers for several minutes until tender, then drain and peel off the skin. Set the bell pepper segments aside while making the yogurt sauce.

Place the avocado and pear in a food processor and purée the ingredients; if the pear is not juicy, it may be necessary to add water, one tablespoon at a time, to make the purée. Push the avocado-pear purée through a fine sieve, then combine it with the yogurt. Fill each bell pepper segment with about 2 tablespoons of the yogurt sauce, cover and refrigerate for 2 to 3 hours.

Remove the plastic wrap from the fish and serve each person a poached redfish fillet accompanied by a stuffed red and yellow bell pepper segment.

4 redfish fillets, about 6 ounces each (Tilapia, drum or trout can be substituted.)

12 large fresh spinach leaves, stemmed and washed

12 large iceberg lettuce leaves, washed

24 medium shrimp, peeled and deveined

1 red bell pepper, seeded and quartered

1 yellow bell pepper, seeded and quartered

1 ripe avocado, peeled and seeded

1 ripe pear, peeled, cored and diced

1 cup plain yogurt

TROUT AMANDINE

4 Servings

---

4 trout fillets, 6 to 8
    ounces each (Tilapia,
    drum or redfish can
    be substituted.)

---

1 large egg

¼ cup milk

All-purpose flour for dredging

---

1 cup almonds, finely
    chopped

½ cup (1 stick) plus
    2 tablespoons butter

Juice of 2 lemons

---

3 tablespoons
    Worcestershire sauce

---

1 tablespoon chopped
    fresh parsley

Salt and black pepper

---

*S*eason the trout fillets on both sides with salt and pepper. In a shallow bowl or pan, beat the egg with the milk. Dredge the fish in the flour, then dip in the egg wash. Coat each fillet with chopped almonds.

Melt ½ cup butter in a large skillet and cook the fish about 4 minutes per side over medium heat until golden brown. Transfer the fillets to a platter and place in a warm oven while preparing the sauce.

To the skillet, add the lemon juice, Worcestershire, parsley, and remaining 2 tablespoons butter. Warm the sauce over low heat and pour over the trout.

Trout Blangé

Melt the butter in a large skillet and cook the onion, bell pepper, and garlic about 2 minutes over medium heat. Add the oysters, shrimp, and saffron and cook another minute. Stir in the tomatoes, paprika, and ¼ cup of the fish stock; cook the mixture for 10 to 15 minutes.

In a small bowl, blend the cornstarch with 2 tablespoons water. Stir the liquid cornstarch into the sauce, season with salt and pepper to taste and cook over moderately high heat until slightly thickened. Sprinkle the Blangé sauce with parsley and keep warm while preparing the fish.

Heat the remaining 2 cups of fish stock in a large sauté pan to just below the boiling point. Poach the trout fillets in the stock about 5 minutes until flaky, then drain on a clean cloth.

Preheat a broiler.

Spoon Blangé sauce onto a warm platter and top with the trout fillets. Cover the trout with additional Blangé sauce, then pipe mashed potatoes around the edge of the platter. Sprinkle the potatoes with paprika and broil until lightly browned.

4 Servings

½ cup (1 stick) butter

¼ cup chopped onion

¼ cup chopped green bell pepper

1 tablespoon minced garlic

18 shucked oysters

6 ounces peeled and deveined medium shrimp

½ teaspoon Spanish saffron

2 cups peeled, seeded and diced tomatoes

1 teaspoon paprika

2¼ cups fish stock (see Index)

1 tablespoon cornstarch

2 tablespoons water

1 tablespoon fresh parsley, finely chopped

4 trout fillets, about 4 ounces each (Tilapia, drum or redfish can be substituted.)

3 cups seasoned mashed potatoes (see Index)

Salt and black pepper

TROUT MEUNIÈRE

4 Servings

4 trout fillets, 6 to 8 ounces
  each (Tilapia, drum or
  redfish can be
  substituted.)

All-purpose flour for dredging

6 *tablespoons butter*

1 *cup lemon butter sauce
  (see Index)*

Salt and black pepper

Berny potatoes (see Index)

Grilled tomatoes (see Index)

Season the trout fillets on both sides with salt and pepper, then dredge in flour.

Melt the butter in a large skillet and sauté the fish until flaky, about 4 minutes per side.

Place a trout fillet on each plate and top with lemon butter sauce. Serve with a berny potato on the side and garnish with a grilled tomato.

TROUT NANCY

Season the trout fillets on both sides with salt and pepper, then dredge in flour. Melt the butter in a large sauté pan and cook the fish over medium heat until flaky, about 4 minutes per side. Remove the fish from the pan and place in a warm oven until serving.

Cook the crabmeat and capers briefly in the pan drippings until hot.

Place a trout fillet on eight plates and top with the crabmeat and capers. Spoon lemon butter sauce over the fish and serve.

8 Servings

---

8 trout fillets (Drum, redfish or tilapia can be substituted.)

All-purpose flour for dredging

¼ cup (½ stick) butter

1½ pounds lump crabmeat, picked over to remove any shell or cartilage (Blanched crawfish tails can be substituted.)

½ cup capers

1½ cups lemon butter sauce (see Index)

Salt and black pepper

TROUT PECAN

4 Servings

---

4 trout fillets, 4 to 6 ounces
    each (Tilapia, drum
    and redfish can be
    substituted.)
    (see note below)

All-purpose flour for dredging

¼ cup (½ stick) plus 3
    tablespoons butter

---

4 ounces lump crabmeat,
    picked over to remove
    any shell and cartilage

---

1 tablespoon
    Worcestershire sauce

---

1 cup chopped pecans

Salt and black pepper

---

*S*eason the trout fillets on both sides with salt and pepper, then dredge in flour. Melt ¼ cup butter in a large sauté pan and cook the fish over medium heat until flaky, about 4 minutes per side. Place the trout in a warm oven until serving.

Drain the excess butter from the pan and add the crabmeat; warm over low heat.

Melt the remaining 3 tablespoons butter in a small saucepan. Drain off the liquid, leaving the butter residue in the pan. Add the Worcestershire and pecans and cook over moderately high heat for 2 minutes.

Place a trout fillet on four plates and top with crabmeat and pecan sauce.

Note: Four lightly pounded veal escalopes, 4 to 6 ounces each, can be substituted for the trout.

FROG LEGS EN CROÛTE

Sever the frog legs at the joint and marinate the legs for 2 hours in the buttermilk.

Melt the butter in a large skillet and sauté the shallots, scallions, and garlic until tender. Stir in the brandy and Worcestershire, then place the frog legs in the pan and cook for 4 minutes over medium heat. Season the mixture with salt and pepper, remove from the heat and let cool for 5 minutes.

Cut the sheets of puff pastry in two and spread on a lightly floured work surface. On each sheet of pastry, place 1 tablespoon of garlic butter, then top with 4 frog legs and one-quarter of the shallot mixture. Fold the pastry over the frog legs so that the seam is underneath. Make four puff pastry packets in all. In a small bowl, beat the egg with milk. Brush the tops of the puff pastry packets with the egg wash, then bake in the hot oven until golden brown, about 25 minutes. Coat the bottom of each serving plate with 2 tablespoons of lemon butter sauce. Set the pastry-wrapped frog legs in the center of the plate and serve.

4 Servings

8	pairs frog legs
2	cups buttermilk
¼	cup (½ stick) butter
4	shallots, finely chopped
¼	cup scallions, finely chopped
2	tablespoons minced garlic
2	tablespoons brandy
½	teaspoon Worcestershire sauce

Two 14 x 11-inch sheets of puff pastry

¼	cup garlic butter (see Index)
1	large egg
¼	cup milk

Salt and black pepper

½	cup lemon butter sauce (see Index)

Preheat oven to 375 degrees F.

Frog Legs Provençale

4 Servings

½ cup (1 stick) butter

½ cup chopped onion

¼ cup chopped green bell
pepper

½ cup sliced mushrooms

---

2 tablespoons chopped
scallions

---

2 teaspoons minced garlic

---

2 cups peeled, seeded, and
diced fresh tomato

---

1 teaspoon Italian
seasoning

---

1 tablespoon brandy

---

16 pairs frog legs

---

1 large egg

¼ cup milk

All-purpose flour for dredging

---

2 cups seasoned bread
crumbs

½ cup vegetable oil

Salt and black pepper

---

*M*elt the butter in a large skillet, then sauté the onions for several minutes until tender. Add the bell pepper, mushrooms, and scallions; sauté briefly. Stir in the garlic, tomato, and Italian seasoning. Season with salt and pepper to taste, then carefully add the brandy. Reduce the heat and simmer the mixture while preparing the frog legs.

Sever the frog legs at the joint and sprinkle with salt and pepper. In a shallow bowl or pan, beat the egg with the milk. Dredge the frog legs in the flour, dip them in the egg wash, then roll in the bread crumbs.

Heat the oil in a skillet and fry the frog legs over medium heat about 5 minutes until golden brown on both sides.

Divide the frog legs between four warm plates. Top with sauce and serve.

CHICKEN À LA BLAKE

In a medium saucepan, bring 3 cups of salted water to a boil. Add the chicken livers and cook for 5 to 7 minutes. Drain and dice the livers, then set them aside.

Season the chicken breasts on both sides with salt and pepper. Melt the butter in a large skillet and sauté the chicken breasts about 8 to 10 minutes until cooked through, turning them once. Transfer the chicken to a platter and place in a warm oven.

Drain all but 2 tablespoons drippings from the skillet. Place the green bell pepper, red bell pepper, onion, scallions, mushrooms, and chicken livers in the pan and sauté the ingredients for 5 minutes, stirring constantly. Add the brandy and green peppercorns to the skillet and flame the mixture.

Place the chicken breasts on four plates and serve with the vegetable mixture on the side.

4 Servings

8	ounces chicken livers
3	cups salted water
4	whole boneless, skinless chicken breasts
½	cup (1 stick) butter
½	cup julienned green bell pepper
½	cup julienned red bell pepper
½	cup sliced onion
½	cup julienned scallions
1	cup sliced mushrooms
¼	cup brandy
1	tablespoon green peppercorns
	Salt and black pepper

CHICKEN CLEMENÇEAU

4 Servings

2 medium Idaho potatoes

Oil for deep frying

¼ cup (½ stick) butter

4 whole boneless, skinless
chicken breasts
(see note below)

1 pound mushrooms,
cleaned and sliced

3 tablespoons garlic, finely
chopped

2 cups scallions, finely
chopped

2 cups cooked green peas

4 teaspoons fresh parsley,
finely chopped

½ cup dry white wine

1 teaspoon salt

½ teaspoon black pepper

4 Holland rusks

Peel and dice the potatoes, then deep fry them in oil heated to 350 degrees F. until tender, about 8 to 10 minutes. Drain the fried potatoes on paper towels while preparing the remainder of the dish.

Melt the butter in a large skillet and cook the chicken breasts over moderately high heat until cooked through, about 4 to 5 minutes per side. Remove the cooked breasts from the pan, keeping them warm until serving.

To the skillet, add the mushrooms, garlic, and scallions. Sauté the vegetables until tender, stirring them frequently, but gently. Add the remaining ingredients, including the fried potatoes, and cook an additional 4 to 6 minutes, until the ingredients are hot.

Place a Holland rusk on each plate, and top with a chicken breast. Spoon a generous portion of sauce and vegetables over the chicken and serve.

Note: Another version of this dish, Shrimp Clemençeau, can be prepared using fresh medium shrimp that have been peeled and deveined. Follow the same procedure, cooking the shrimp in butter for several minutes until they turn pink.

CHICKEN FLORENTINE

✥

$\mathcal{M}$elt the butter in a large skillet, and cook the chicken breasts over moderately high heat until cooked through, about 4 to 5 minutes per side. Remove the chicken from the pan and slice the breast in half. Set the chicken aside while preparing the sauce.

Over medium heat, whisk the flour into the pan drippings. Gradually incorporate the milk into the flour, stirring constantly until smooth and thick enough to coat the back of a spoon. Add the Parmesan cheese and season to taste with salt and pepper. Reduce the heat and simmer the sauce another 2 minutes. Adjust the consistency with additional milk if the sauce seems too thick.

Cover the bottoms of four ovenproof serving plates with creamed spinach. Top the spinach with the chicken, then pour cream sauce over the breasts.

Fill a pastry bag fitted with a large plain tip with mashed potatoes and pipe mashed potatoes around the chicken, along the edge of the plate. Sprinkle the potatoes with paprika and broil until lightly browned; serve immediately.

4 Servings

¼ cup (½ stick) butter
4 whole boneless, skinless chicken breasts
2 tablespoons all-purpose flour
1 cup scalded milk
2 tablespoons freshly grated Parmesan cheese
4 cups creamed spinach (see Index)
4 cups mashed potatoes Randolph (see Index)
1 teaspoon paprika
Salt and white pepper

CHICKEN CORSICA

---

2 cups chicken stock
(see Index)

---

1 cup water

---

4 whole boneless, skinless
chicken breasts

---

2 tablespoons red wine
vinegar

---

2 tablespoons Italian
seasoning

---

20 asparagus spears,
steamed or blanched
until tender

---

2 cups fresh spinach
leaves, stemmed and
washed

Cream Sauce (recipe follows)

---

1 pound boiled angel hair
pasta

Combine the chicken stock and 1 cup of water in a large sauté pan; heat the liquid to just below the boiling point.

Brush the chicken breasts on both sides with the vinegar, then sprinkle with the Italian seasoning. Spread the chicken breasts on a flat work surface and top each breast with 5 asparagus spears and ½ cup spinach leaves. Roll the breasts and wrap them tightly in aluminum foil. Place the foil packets in the simmering chicken stock and water; poach for 10 to 12 minutes, turning occasionally, until the chicken is cooked through. Remove the pan from the heat and let the chicken remain in the stock while preparing the sauce.

Remove the aluminum foil and slice the breasts into medallions. Serve the chicken roulades over boiled pasta, topped with cream sauce.

CREAM SAUCE

$\mathcal{M}$elt the butter in a large sauté pan, then blend in the flour. Cook over medium heat, stirring constantly, until the mixture is golden brown. Whisk in the chicken stock, then add the asparagus, Italian seasoning, and cream. Lower the heat and simmer the sauce for 6 to 8 minutes until thickened. Season to taste with salt and pepper.

Note: For a plain cream sauce, the asparagus and Italian seasoning can be omitted.

½ cup (1 stick) butter

½ cup all-purpose flour

1 cup chicken stock
   (see Index)

6 asparagus spears,
   steamed or blanched
   until tender and diced

Pinch of Italian seasoning

½ cup heavy cream

Salt and white pepper to taste

CHICKEN LAZONE

4 Servings

1 teaspoon salt (or less to taste)

1½ teaspoons chili powder

1½ teaspoons onion powder

2 teaspoons garlic powder

4 whole boneless, skinless chicken breasts

¼ cup (½ stick) butter

½ cup heavy cream

In a small bowl, combine the salt, chili powder, onion powder, and garlic powder. Coat the chicken breasts with the seasoning mixture.

Melt 2 tablespoons of the butter in a large sauté pan, then cook the chicken breasts over medium heat about 7 to 8 minutes, turning them once. Pour the cream into the pan and lower the heat. Simmer for several minutes, stirring, until the sauce thickens, then fold in the remaining 2 tablespoons butter. When the butter is melted, transfer the chicken breasts to four plates and top with the sauce.

CHICKEN PONTALBA

⚜

4 Servings

$\mathcal{P}$eel and dice the potato, then pan or deep-fry until golden brown. Drain the diced potato on paper towels and set aside while preparing the chicken.

Season the chicken breasts on both sides with salt and pepper, then dredge in the flour. Melt the butter in a large skillet and sauté the chicken until tender and golden brown, about 4 minutes per side. Transfer the breasts to a covered baking dish and place in a warm oven.

In the pan drippings, sauté the onion, garlic, mushrooms, and ham. When the vegetables are tender, add the scallions, potatoes, parsley, and wine. Season with salt and pepper, then simmer the mixture until the ingredients are heated through.

Place the chicken breasts on four plates and spoon the vegetable mixture on the side. Top the chicken with béarnaise and serve.

1	*small Idaho potato*
4	*whole boneless, skinless chicken breasts*
	All-purpose flour for dredging
½	*cup (1 stick) butter*
1	*cup onion, finely chopped*
2	*tablespoons minced garlic*
1	*cup thinly sliced mushrooms*
1	*cup ham, finely chopped*
1	*cup chopped scallions*
¼	*cup chopped fresh parsley*
½	*cup dry white wine*
	Salt and black pepper
1	*cup béarnaise sauce (see Index)*

CHICKEN ROCHAMBEAU

4 Servings

---

1 *quart chicken stock*
(see Index)

---

4 *whole boneless, skinless*
chicken breasts

---

8 *Holland rusks*

---

8 *slices Canadian bacon*
or ham

---

3 *cups marchand de vin*
sauce (see Index)

---

1 *cup béarnaise sauce*
(see Index)

Grilled tomatoes for garnish
(see Index)

Preheat oven to 350 degrees F.

$\mathscr{A}$rrange the chicken breasts in a 9 x 13-inch baking dish. Pour the chicken stock over the breasts and bake in the hot oven until the breasts are tender and cooked through, about 30 minutes.

Place 2 Holland rusks on each plate and top with slices of Canadian bacon or ham; cover with marchand de vin sauce. Center the breasts on the plates, spoon béarnaise over the chicken and garnish with grilled tomatoes.

Chicken And Sausage Jambalaya

❧

*M*elt the butter in a large ovenproof saucepan or Dutch oven. Add the onion, bell pepper, celery, and garlic and cook over moderately high heat until tender. Stir in the scallions, chicken, and sausage. Sauté the mixture an additional 5 minutes, then add the remaining ingredients, except the rice. Reduce the heat to low and simmer for 10 to 15 minutes. Stir in the rice, cover the pan, then place in the hot oven until the rice is tender, about 45 minutes; stir the mixture occasionally during cooking.

Alternatively, the jambalaya may be simmered on the stove top, covered, for 25 to 30 minutes.

Fluff the cooked jambalaya with a fork, remove the bay leaf, then serve.

4 Servings

⅓	cup butter
½	cup chopped onion
½	cup chopped green bell pepper
½	cup chopped celery
1	tablespoon minced garlic
½	cup chopped scallions
1½	cups diced uncooked chicken
1½	cups sliced andouille or other spicy smoked sausage
2	cups fresh or canned whole tomatoes
½	cup tomato paste
1	cup chicken stock (see Index)
1	bay leaf
½	teaspoon salt
¼	teaspoon cayenne pepper
1	cup raw white rice, rinsed

Preheat oven to 350 degrees F.

CHICKEN AND TASSO WITH PASTA BORDELAISE

⌘

6 Servings

8	*cups water*
2	*teaspoons salt*
2	*tablespoons olive oil*
1	*pound capellini pasta*
6	*whole boneless, skinless chicken breasts*
3	*tablespoons butter*
1	*pound diced tasso (see note below)*
2	*teaspoons chopped garlic*
3	*cups heavy cream*
1	*bunch scallions, coarsely chopped*

Salt and black pepper

*B*ring 8 cups of water to a boil, along with 2 teaspoons salt and the olive oil. Place the pasta in the water and when the liquid returns to a boil, cook for 5 minutes, stirring occasionally. Drain the pasta, then plunge the noodles into a container of cold water; let sit for 5 minutes, then drain.

Cut each chicken breast into 4 pieces. Melt the butter in a large skillet, and sauté the chicken pieces over medium heat for several minutes. Add the tasso and garlic, then cook for another 5 minutes. Stir the cream and scallions into the mixture, reduce the heat, and simmer the sauce for 10 minutes. Season to taste with salt and pepper.

Toss the drained pasta in the sauce and serve.

Note: Tasso is highly-seasoned Cajun smoked ham. If unavailable, substitute smoked ham and add cayenne pepper to taste.

POULET BRENNAN

*P*lace the chickens, breast side down, on a cutting board. Make an incision along the spine and split the chickens open. Using a small, sharp knife, bone the breasts and lower portion of the leg, being careful not to pierce the skin as you cut flesh from bone. Rinse the partially boned chickens and pat them dry.

Season the meat inside and out with salt and pepper. Spoon oyster dressing onto the cavity of both chickens, then close the birds and truss with string. Brush the chickens with butter and place on a rack in a large roasting pan. Roast in the hot oven for 45 minutes. Remove the string from the roasted chickens and slice them in half lengthwise. Place one half of a chicken on each plate, top with marchand de vin sauce and serve with sweet potatoes on the side.

4 Servings

2 chickens, 2¼ to 2½ pounds each

3 cups oyster dressing (see Index)

Melted butter for brushing

Salt and black pepper

2 cups marchand de vin sauce (see Index)

Sweet Potatoes (see Index)

Preheat oven to 375 degrees F.

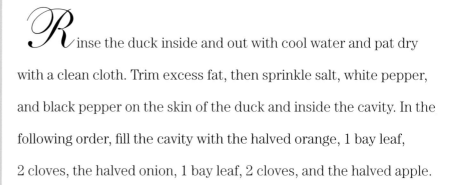

DUCKLING WITH
BLACK CHERRY SAUCE

2 Servings

1	Long Island duckling, about 3 to 4 pounds
½	orange
2	bay leaves
4	cloves
½	small onion
½	apple
	Melted butter for brushing
1	tablespoon all-purpose flour
2	cups chicken stock (see Index)
2	tablespoons red wine
2	teaspoons sugar
1	cup dark cherries with ½ cup cherry juice
2	tablespoons cherry liqueur
	Salt, white pepper, and black pepper

Preheat oven to 450 degrees F.

$\mathcal{R}$inse the duck inside and out with cool water and pat dry with a clean cloth. Trim excess fat, then sprinkle salt, white pepper, and black pepper on the skin of the duck and inside the cavity. In the following order, fill the cavity with the halved orange, 1 bay leaf, 2 cloves, the halved onion, 1 bay leaf, 2 cloves, and the halved apple.

Place the duck in a baking pan and brush with melted butter. Roast in the hot oven for 15 to 20 minutes until the skin is crisp, then reduce the oven heat to 325 degrees F.; continue to cook for 45 minutes to an hour until done to preference. If the juice runs pink when the breast is pierced with a skewer, the meat is rare. If the breast juice runs clear, the duck is cooked to well-done.

Remove the duck to a platter and drain the fat from the roasting pan. Blend the flour into the remaining drippings, scraping any brown crust from the bottom of the pan. Whisk in the chicken stock and bring the mixture to a rolling boil. Reduce over moderately high heat for 5 minutes, then remove from the heat.

In a saucepan, whisk the red wine and sugar over medium heat. When the sugar dissolves, add the cherry juice and cook for 5 minutes. Strain the pan drippings into the cherry mixture and reduce the sauce until thick enough to coat a spoon. Stir in the cherries and cherry liqueur and simmer 1 to 2 minutes.

Remove the seasonings from the cavity and cut the duck in half lengthwise. Remove the wings and partially bone the duck. If desired, serve the duck on a bed of rice seasoned with sautéed onion and carrot. Spoon black cherry sauce over the duck and stud with cherries.

ROASTED QUAIL IN A POTATO BASKET WITH WILD RICE

4 Servings

½ cup (1 stick) butter
½ cup onion, finely chopped
½ cup diced mushrooms
1 bay leaf
1½ teaspoons thyme leaves
Pinch of cayenne pepper
¼ cup all-purpose flour
1½ cups chicken stock (see Index)
2 tablespoons Worcestershire sauce
1½ teaspoons garlic, finely chopped
½ cup dry red wine
¼ cup chopped scallions
1 cup diced carrots
¼ cup fresh parsley, finely chopped
4 quail, about 5 ounces each
4 strips of bacon
Salt and black pepper
4 potato baskets (recipe follows)
Wild rice (recipe follows)

Melt the butter in a large saucepan and sauté the onion until tender. Add the mushrooms, bay leaf, thyme, and cayenne; season with salt and pepper, then stir in the flour. When the mixture is well blended, add the chicken stock, Worcestershire, garlic, wine, scallions, and carrots. Simmer the sauce for 1 hour, then remove the bay leaf and stir in the parsley. Remove from the heat and keep warm until serving.

Preheat oven to 375 degrees F.

Season the quail with salt and pepper and wrap with a strip of bacon. Place the quail, breast side up in a baking dish and roast in the hot oven for 15 to 20 minutes until done.

Spoon a bed of wild rice onto each serving plate and set the potato basket on top of the rice. Place the quail in the potato basket and spoon the warm sauce over the quail.

POTATO BASKETS

❧

$\mathcal{P}$eel and shred the potatoes into thin strips. Line a small wire mesh strainer with one-quarter of the potato strips and fit a second strainer, slightly smaller than the first, over the potatoes. Deep fry the potato baskets one at a time in oil heated to 390 degrees F. Cook until golden, about 5 minutes, then separate the strainers and carefully remove the potato baskets. Drain on paper towels, then serve.

4 medium Idaho potatoes

Oil for deep frying

WILD RICE BLEND

❧

$\mathcal{C}$ook the wild rice until tender according to the package directions. Melt the butter in a large skillet and sauté the scallions, pecans, and ham until the ham is lightly browned. Add the remaining ingredients and cook over medium heat, stirring, for 5 minutes. Fold in the wild rice and serve.

1 cup wild rice blend

1 tablespoon butter

⅓ cup chopped scallions

½ cup minced ham

⅓ cup chopped pecans

¼ cup fresh parsley, finely chopped

1 tablespoon white wine

½ teaspoon white pepper

Salt to taste

PAN ROASTED QUAIL AND GREEN PEPPERCORNS

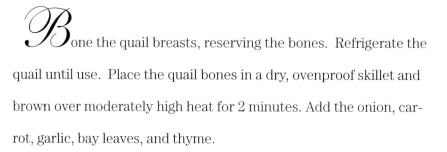

6 Servings

6 quail, 5 to 6 ounces each
1 small onion, diced
1 medium carrot, diced
6 garlic cloves
2 bay leaves
1/4 teaspoon thyme leaves
4 ripe pears
1/2 cup beef stock (see Index)
1 1/2 cups water
All-purpose flour for dusting
2 tablespoons butter
1 large yellow bell pepper, finely julienned
1 large red bell pepper, finely julienned
2 tablespoons green peppercorns
1/4 teaspoon sugar
1 cup port wine

Preheat oven to 400 degrees F.

Bone the quail breasts, reserving the bones. Refrigerate the quail until use. Place the quail bones in a dry, ovenproof skillet and brown over moderately high heat for 2 minutes. Add the onion, carrot, garlic, bay leaves, and thyme.

Peel and chop one of the pears; set the other pears aside. Stir the chopped pear into the quail bone mixture, then roast in the hot oven for 10 minutes. Remove the pan from the oven and add the beef stock and 1½ cups of water to the bones. Reduce over low heat about 15 minutes to yield 1 cup of quail stock. Strain the stock and set it aside. Preheat oven to 375 degrees F.

Dust the skin of the quail with flour. Melt the butter in an ovenproof skillet and sauté the quail, skin side down, until browned. Place the skillet in the oven and roast the quail for 6 minutes, turning them once. Transfer the quail to a platter. Peel the remaining 3 pears and cut them into thin slices. Drain the fat from the pan, then add the sliced pear, along with the yellow and red bell peppers.

Cook the mixture over high heat about 2 minutes, stirring constantly. Add the green peppercorns and the strained quail stock. Lower the heat to medium and cook until the pears and bell peppers are tender and the stock is almost evaporated, about 15 minutes. Return the quail to the pan and add the sugar and wine. Cook briefly, until the wine is hot, then carefully ignite the mixture. Simmer, stirring, until the alcohol is cooked out and the flames subside, remove the bay leaves, then spoon a bed of the green peppercorn mixture onto six plates. Place one quail in the center of each plate and serve.

Pork Chops Stuffed With Oyster Dressing

❧

*M*elt the butter in a large skillet and sauté the onion, celery, bell pepper, and garlic. When the vegetables are tender, add the bay leaf, thyme, Worcestershire, and oysters, along with any oyster water. Cook for 2 to 3 minutes, until the edges of the oysters begin to curl. Season the mixture with salt and pepper to taste, then working quickly stir in the egg. Fold in the bread crumbs and parsley and cook for 1 to 2 minutes longer until the mixture is heated through.

Cut a pocket in the eye of each chop and gently pound the flaps over the edge of a cutting board. Spoon stuffing into the pork chops, close the flaps and secure with toothpicks. Sprinkle the pork chops on both sides with pepper.

Preheat oven to 375 degrees F.

Melt 2 tablespoons butter in another large skillet and sear the pork chops on both sides. Pour ¼ cup beef stock or water into the pan and bake in the hot oven about 20 minutes until fully cooked.

Place any leftover dressing into a buttered baking dish and place in the oven with the pork chops.

6 Servings

½ cup (1 stick) plus
    2 tablespoons butter

½ cup onion, finely chopped

½ cup celery, finely chopped

½ cup green bell pepper,
    finely chopped

2 tablespoons minced
    garlic

1 large bay leaf

Pinch of thyme

1 tablespoon
    Worcestershire sauce

24 shucked oysters

1 large egg

2 cups seasoned bread
    crumbs

1 tablespoon fresh parsley,
    finely chopped

6 thick, center cut pork
    chops, about 8 ounces
    each

¼ cup beef stock or water

Salt and black pepper

Sweet Potatoes (see Index)

Tenderloin Of Pork Stuffed With Wild Rice, Andouille And Pecans

4 Servings

- *¼ cup (½ stick) butter*
- *¾ cup onion, finely chopped*
- *½ cup green bell pepper, finely chopped*
- *¼ cup celery, finely chopped*
- *¾ cup diced andouille (Spicy smoked sausage can be substituted.)*
- *1 tablespoon minced garlic*
- *1 teaspoon thyme leaves*
- *¼ cup dry white wine*
- *½ cup chopped scallions*
- *¼ cup chopped pecans*
- *1 cup cooked wild rice*
- *½ cup seasoned bread crumbs*
- *3 pounds pork tenderloin, trimmed of fat and silverskin*
- *½ cup port wine*
- *Salt and black pepper*

Melt 2 tablespoons of the butter in a large skillet and cook the onion, bell pepper, and celery until tender. Add the andouille, garlic, and thyme. Season with salt and pepper, then cook about 8 minutes over medium heat. Stir in the white wine, scallions, pecans, wild rice, and bread crumbs. Fill a pastry bag with the stuffing and set it aside while preparing the pork.

Cut the tenderloin in two and using a long, sharp knife make a slit in the center of both pieces, forming a pocket in each. Insert the handle of a wooden spoon to enlarge the opening. Working from either end of the pieces of tenderloin, pipe stuffing into the pocket until full.

Preheat oven to 350 degrees F.

Melt the remaining 2 tablespoons butter in a large, ovenproof sauté pan and sear the stuffed tenderloin. Deglaze the pan with port wine and roast in the hot oven about 45 minutes until done.

Remove the tenderloin from the pan and slice into medallions. Reduce the stock in the pan by half, spoon over the pork and serve.

VEAL ALANA MICHELLE

Season the veal on both sides with salt and pepper, then dust with flour. Melt the butter in a large sauté pan and cook the escalopes over moderately high heat about 3 minutes per side. Add the crabmeat to the pan and cook for 1 to 2 minutes until warmed through.

Place the veal escalopes on four serving plates and top with crabmeat and béarnaise.

4 Servings

4 veal escalopes, 4 to 6 ounces each, lightly pounded

All-purpose flour for dusting

3 tablespoons butter

4 ounces lump crabmeat, picked over to remove any shell and cartilage (Blanched crawfish tails can be substituted.)

1 cup béarnaise sauce (see index)

Salt and black pepper

DOUBLE VEAL CHOP TASTEVIN

Preheat a grill. Press the cracked black peppercorns onto both sides of the veal chops, then sear on the hot grill until scored with grill marks on both sides.

Place the seared chops in a rectangular baking dish and add the butter and ¼ cup water. Roast the chops in the hot oven for 20 to 30 minutes until medium or well done. Transfer the veal chops to warm plates and add the parsley to the pan drippings; drizzle the drippings over the meat.

If desired, serve the veal chops accompanied by a colorful array of sautéed vegetables, such as baby zucchini, sunburst squash, green beans, and new potatoes.

4 Servings

2 tablespoons cracked black peppercorns

4 white veal chops, about 16 ounces each

2 tablespoons butter

¼ cup water

1 tablespoon chopped fresh parsley

Preheat oven to 400 degrees F.

VEAL CARDINAL

8 Servings

2	large eggs
½	cup milk
8	veal escalopes, 4 to 6 ounces each, lightly pounded
2	cups seasoned bread crumbs
½	cup (1 stick) butter
1½	cups ketchup
¾	cup sour cream

Juice of ½ lemon

1	tablespoon Worcestershire sauce

Pinch of white pepper

Salt and black pepper

In a shallow bowl or pan, beat the egg with the milk. Season the veal with salt and pepper, then dip in the egg wash. Coat the escalopes with bread crumbs.

Melt the butter in a large sauté pan and cook the veal over moderately high heat until golden brown, about 3 minutes per side. Remove the veal from the pan and place in a warm oven while preparing the sauce.

Place the ketchup in a medium saucepan and cook over low heat. Gradually whisk the sour cream into the ketchup, then add the remaining ingredients. Cook the sauce until hot, stirring it frequently.

Place a veal escalope on each plate and top with the sauce.

VEAL KOTTWITZ

Season the veal with salt and pepper. Melt the butter in a large sauté pan and cook the escalopes over moderately high heat about 3 minutes per side. Remove the veal from the pan and place in a warm oven until serving.

Combine the sliced artichoke bottoms and mushrooms in the sauté pan. Add the wine, then cook the mixture for 5 minutes over medium heat. Blend in the lemon butter sauce and warm gently.

Serve the veal topped with the artichoke-mushroom mixture.

Note: Four trout fillets, (tilapia, drum or redfish), 4 to 6 ounces each, can be substituted for the veal escalopes.

6 Servings

6 *veal escalopes, 4 to 6 ounces each, lightly pounded (see note below)*
6 *tablespoons butter*
28 *ounces artichoke bottoms, sliced*
1 *pound sliced mushrooms*
2 *tablespoons dry white wine*
1 *cup lemon butter sauce (see Index)*
Salt and black pepper

VEAL MONYA

8 Servings

¾	cup (1½ sticks) butter
1	cup onion, finely chopped
½	cup all-purpose flour plus extra for dusting
1	quart chicken stock (see Index)
½	cup heavy cream
½	cup Madeira
8	veal escalopes, 4 to 6 ounces each, lightly pounded (see note below)
1	tablespoon Parmesan cheese

Salt and white pepper

*M*elt ¼ cup of the butter in a skillet and sauté the onion about 5 minutes until tender. Blend in the flour and cook about 2 minutes, then pour in the chicken stock. Whisk the mixture until smooth and cook about 15 minutes over medium heat. Stir in the heavy cream and Madeira, then reduce the sauce until thickened. Season to taste with salt and white pepper.

While the sauce is reducing, prepare the veal. Season the escalopes with salt and pepper, then dust with flour. Melt the remaining ½ cup butter in a large sauté pan and cook the veal over moderately high heat about 3 minutes per side.

Serve the veal on warm plates, topped with the Madeira cream sauce. Top with 1 tablespoon parmesan cheese and broil until the cheese melts, about 1 to 2 minutes. Serve immediately.

Note: Chicken breasts can be substituted for the veal escalopes.

VEAL WITH MOREL MUSHROOMS

✀

*I*n a stainless steel or glass bowl, combine ½ cup of the Madeira with 2 cups water. Place the morels in the liquid and marinate at room temperature for 15 minutes. Strain off the marinade. Drain the mushrooms, then quarter or halve each cap, depending on its size.

Melt ¼ cup of the butter in a medium skillet and sauté the onion until tender, about 5 minutes. Reduce the heat to medium and blend in the flour. Cook for 2 to 3 minutes, then pour in the chicken stock. Whisk the mixture until smooth and cook for 15 minutes over low heat, stirring frequently. Stir in the cream, the remaining ½ cup Madeira and the morel mushrooms. Reduce the sauce until thickened, then adjust the seasoning with salt and white pepper.

While the sauce is reducing, season the veal escalopes on both sides with salt and pepper, then dust with flour. Melt the remaining ½ cup butter in a large sauté pan and cook the veal over moderately high heat about 3 minutes per side.

Serve the veal on warm plates topped with the Madeira-morel cream sauce.

Note: Chicken breasts can be substituted for the veal escalopes.

8 Servings

1 cup Madeira

2 cups water

24 morel mushrooms

¾ cup (1½ sticks) butter

1 cup onion, finely chopped

½ cup all-purpose flour, plus extra for dusting

1 quart chicken stock (see Index)

½ cup heavy cream

8 veal escalopes, 4 to 6 ounces each, lightly pounded (see note below)

Salt and white pepper

OSSO BUCCO

4 Servings

---

4 thick veal shanks, 6 to 8 ounces each
All-purpose flour for dusting
1 cup vegetable oil
1 cup chopped onion
3 garlic cloves, minced
1½ cups diced tomato
1 cup dry white wine
1 cup beef stock (see Index)
¼ cup fresh parsley, finely chopped
Salt and black pepper

Preheat oven to 350 degrees F.

Sprinkle the veal shanks on both sides with salt and pepper, then dust with flour. Heat the oil until almost smoking in a Dutch oven or roasting pan. Sear the veal shanks on both sides until brown, then remove them from the pan and set aside.

Drain all but ¼ cup of the oil from the pan, then return the pan to medium heat. Add the onion, garlic, and tomato, and cook the mixture for 3 to 4 minutes; do not let the onions brown. Stir in the wine, stock, and parsley, then season with salt and pepper to taste. Place the veal shanks on top of the vegetable mixture. Cover and roast in the hot oven for 1 hour, until the meat is tender.

Serve the veal shanks over angel hair pasta or rice, topped with the tomato mixture.

CROWN ROAST OF LAMB WITH VEGETABLES

*R*ub the lamb roast inside and out with the lemon juice, 1 teaspoon salt, 1 teaspoon pepper, and the thyme. Pour 4 tablespoons olive oil in the center of the roast, then cover the tips of the bones with foil to prevent burning. Place the lamb on a rack in a roasting pan, arrange the new potatoes around the roast, and bake in the hot oven for 1½ hours.

Wash the okra in cold running water and trim the stems. Place the okra in a bowl and cover with vinegar. Let stand for 30 minutes at room temperature, then drain.

Combine 2 tablespoons olive oil and the butter in a large skillet. Add the onions and cook over medium heat until golden brown. Stir in the corn, tomatoes, marinated okra, and sugar. Season the mixture with salt and pepper to taste, then simmer the mixture for 15 minutes.

Remove the roast from the oven and take the crown out of the pan. Pour the okra mixture into the bottom of the pan, then place the lamb back in the pan, on top of the vegetables. Cover and return the pan to the oven for an additional 30 minutes.

To serve, transfer the crown roast to a platter and remove the foil from bones. Spoon the okra mixture into the center of the crown and around the base. Scatter potatoes around the platter and, if desired, serve with natural juices or mint jelly.

1	crown roast of spring lamb, about 16 chops
¼	cup lemon juice
1	teaspoon salt
1	teaspoon black pepper
1	teaspoon thyme
6	tablespoons olive oil
2	pounds new potatoes, scrubbed and halved
1	pound okra
3	cups red wine vinegar
½	cup (1 stick) butter
1¾	cups onion, finely chopped
4	cups fresh corn kernels
3	large ripe tomatoes, seeded and chopped
½	teaspoon sugar
	Salt and black pepper

Preheat oven to 350 degrees F.

4 racks of lamb, about
1 pound each

Salt and black pepper

3 large eggs

½ cup milk

1 cup all-purpose flour

1 cup seasoned bread crumbs

Vegetable oil for deep frying

Mint Sauce (recipe follows)

Chime bones and trimmings
reserved from lamb racks

1 tablespoon vegetable oil

¼ cup diced carrots

¼ cup diced celery

¼ cup parsley, finely chopped

1 teaspoon minced garlic

1 teaspoon thyme leaves

2 bay leaves

1½ tablespoons flour

3 cups water

½ cup (4 ounces) mint or
apple mint jelly

Preheat oven to 400 degrees F.

BABY LAMB CHOPS GRAND DUKE ALEXIS

*R*emove the chime bone (backbone) from each rack and trim the fat and sinew (silverskin); reserve the bones and trimmings for the mint sauce. Cut the racks into individual chops by slicing between the rib bones. Season the lamb chops with salt and pepper.

Combine the eggs and milk in a shallow bowl and beat until well blended. Dust the lamb chops in flour, dip them in the egg wash, then dredge them in bread crumbs. Fry the chops in batches in deep fat that has been heated to 350 degrees; fry 4 to 5 minutes, until golden brown.

Drain the chops briefly on paper towels, then divide them between four dinner plates, fanning them around the plate. Place a small dish of mint sauce in the center of each plate and serve.

MINT SAUCE

*C*ombine all of the ingredients except the flour and jelly in a 6-quart cast iron or other heavy ovenproof pot. Lightly brown the reserved bones over high heat on top of the stove, then transfer the pan to the hot oven. Roast the bones and vegetables until very dark brown, about 30 minutes; do not allow the ingredients to burn.

Stir the flour into the mixture and cook an additional 5 to 6 minutes in the oven. Remove the pot from the oven and place over high heat on top of the stove. Stir in 3 cups of water, then reduce about 20 minutes, stirring frequently, until thick enough to coat the back of a spoon. Strain the sauce into a large saucepan and add the mint jelly. Simmer over low heat for 10 minutes, then serve warm. Mint sauce can be made ahead of time and refrigerated; warm gently before serving.

BABY RACK OF LAMB BOUQUETIÈRE

Season the racks with salt and pepper and place on a baking sheet. Broil the lamb for 5 to 7 minutes until browned.

Preheat oven to 375 degrees. F.

Spread garlic butter on the racks and sprinkle with bread crumbs. Roast the lamb in the hot oven about 45 minutes until done to preference. Remove the racks from the oven and cut between the bones into chops.

Place the chops on a serving platter and top with either béarnaise or marchand de vin sauce. Arrange the cooked vegetables around the lamb and serve.

4 Servings

4 racks of lamb, about 1 pound each

½ teaspoon salt

½ teaspoon black pepper

½ cup garlic butter (see Index)

½ cup seasoned bread crumbs

1 cup béarnaise or marchand de vin sauce (see Index)

Any combination of steamed cauliflower, broccoli, asparagus or grilled tomatoes for garnish

Preheat a broiler.

LAMB CHOPS MIRABEAU

Sprinkle the lamb with salt and pepper, then grill or broil the chops until done to preference.

Heat the tomato sauce gently and spoon 2 tablespoons of warm tomato sauce onto four plates. Crisscross 2 lamb chops in the center of each plate, then cover the eye of the chops with béarnaise sauce. Surround the lamb chops with the bacon strips and serve.

4 Servings

8 lamb chops

4 ounces (½ cup) tomato sauce

1 cup béarnaise sauce (see Index)

12 strips of crisp cooked bacon

Salt and black pepper

Preheat a grill or broiler.

BEEF WELLINGTON

4 to 6 Servings

1½ pounds beef tenderloin, whole, trimmed, and peeled

¼ cup (½ stick) plus 1 teaspoon butter

½ cup scallions, finely chopped

1 cup chopped mushrooms

8 ounces Créole Liver Pâté (see Index)

2 tablespoons minced garlic

½ cup fresh parsley, finely chopped

1 large egg

½ cup milk

1 14 x 11-inch sheet of puff pastry

Salt and black pepper

Madeira sauce (recipe follows)

*M*elt 1 teaspoon of butter in a skillet and sear the outside of the tenderloin until brown; do not cook the inside. Set the meat aside while preparing the duxelles seasoning mixture.

Melt the remaining ¼ cup butter in a large skillet and sauté the scallions and mushrooms for 4 minutes. Stir in the pâté, garlic, and parsley and adjust the seasoning with salt and pepper to taste.

Preheat oven to 350 degrees F.

In a small bowl, beat the egg with the milk. Spread the sheet of puff pastry on a flat work surface and brush with the egg wash. Spread the duxelles mixture down the center of the dough and set the tenderloin on top. Wrap the dough around the meat with the seam on the bottom; fold the ends under. Brush the surface of the pastry with egg wash and place on a buttered baking sheet, seam side down. Bake in the oven about 40 minutes until the dough is fully baked; if the dough browns too quickly, cover the loaf with aluminum foil.

Remove the beef Wellington from the oven and let it rest for 10 minutes. Slice about ¾-inch thick and serve with Madeira sauce.

MADEIRA SAUCE

✤

Melt the brown sauce in a small saucepan, then add the Madeira. Reduce the sauce over medium heat until thickened. Lower the heat and add the butter, swirling the pan to incorporate it into the sauce.

Yields 1½ cups

1 cup brown sauce
   (see Index)

¾ cup Madeira

1 tablespoon butter

CHÂTEAUBRIAND BOUQUETIÈRE

✤

Sprinkle the beef on both sides with salt and pepper. Place the filet on the hot grill or under the broiler and baste with melted butter. Cook for 15 to 30 minutes until done according to your preference; when the internal temperature reaches 120 degrees, the meat is cooked rare. Slice the beef and serve topped with béarnaise. Garnish with sautéed fresh seasonal vegetables.

4 Servings

2 pounds beef tenderloin

¼ cup (½ stick)
   melted butter

Salt and black pepper

1 cup béarnaise sauce
   (see Index)

Preheat a grill or broiler.

FILET BRENNAN

4 Servings

2 tablespoons butter

½ cup sliced mushrooms

1 tablespoon all-purpose
flour

¼ cup red wine

½ cup beef stock
(see Index)

¼ teaspoon
Worcestershire sauce

4 filets mignons

Salt and black pepper

Grilled tomatoes (see Index)

*M*elt the butter in a small sauté pan and cook the
mushrooms over low heat until tender. Blend in the flour and cook,
stirring, until lightly browned. Stir in the wine, stock, and
Worcestershire. Season the sauce with salt and pepper to taste
and simmer until slightly thickened.

Preheat a grill or broiler.

Sprinkle the steaks with salt and pepper on both sides, then grill or
broil until done to preference.

Place the filets mignons on four warm plates and spoon mushroom
sauce over the meat. Garnish with the grilled tomatoes and serve.

FILET STANLEY

Sprinkle the halved beef filets on both sides with salt and pepper. Grill or broil the meat until done to preference.

In a large skillet, melt the butter and sauté the sliced bananas until tender and lightly browned, about 4 minutes per side.

To serve, place 2 Holland rusks in the center of eight heated plates. Arrange a slice of banana on either side of the rusks near the edge of the plate. Spoon horseradish sauce between the bananas and the rusks. Place a piece of cooked filet on each Holland rusk and top with red wine and mushroom sauce.

HORSERADISH SAUCE

In a saucepan, combine the cream, pepper, and salt. Cook over medium heat, but do not let the cream reach a boil. Blend the butter and flour together and form a small ball. Add the butter ball to the simmering cream. Cook until the sauce is smooth, then add the horseradish. Serve warm.

8 Servings

---

8 *beef filets, about 8 ounces each, halved*

½ *cup (1 stick) butter*

---

8 *bananas, sliced in half lengthwise*

Salt and freshly ground black pepper to taste

---

16 *Holland rusks*

½ *cup horseradish sauce (recipe follows)*

---

2 *cups Brennan's red wine and mushroom sauce (see Index)*

Preheat a grill or broiler.

Yields 1½ cups

---

2 *cups heavy cream*

¼ *teaspoon white pepper*

¼ *teaspoon salt*

¼ *teaspoon butter*

---

2 *tablespoons all-purpose flour*

---

2 *tablespoons horseradish*

BRENNAN'S STEAK DIANE

4 Servings

---

2 tablespoons butter

---

12 beef tournedos, about 3
ounces each

---

2 cups sliced mushrooms

---

1 cup chopped scallions

---

2 cups brown sauce
(see Index)

---

4 tablespoons chopped
fresh parsley

---

*M*elt the butter in a large skillet and sear the meat. Add the mushrooms and scallions to the pan, then cook for 2 minutes over medium heat. Stir in the brown sauce and cook until the mixture is heated through.

Arrange 3 tournedos on each plate and top with the mushroom sauce. Sprinkle parsley over the meat and serve

STEAK AU POIVRE
WITH BARBECUED SHRIMP

❦

With the knife parallel to the work surface, butterfly the beef tournedos; do not cut all the way through the filets. Open the filets and press peppercorns onto both sides of the meat. Grill or broil until done to preference.

Place the tournedos on warm plates and top with pepper sauce. Serve barbecued shrimp on the side of the meat, with slices of French bread.

4 Servings

4 *beef tournedos, 6 to 8 ounces each*

4 *tablespoons cracked black peppercorns*

2 *cups pepper sauce (see Index)*

New Orleans barbecued shrimp (see Index)

Preheat a grill or broiler.

HAMBURGER BRENNAN

6 Servings

2	*pounds ground chuck*
¼	*cup minced scallions*
¼	*cup minced onion*
2	*tablespoons Worcestershire sauce*
1	*tablespoon chopped fresh parsley*
2	*large eggs*

Pinch of nutmeg

1½	*teaspoons salt*
½	*teaspoon black pepper*
1½	*cups sauce maison (recipe follows)*

Preheat a grill or broiler.

*C*ombine all of the ingredients in a large bowl. When the mixture is well combined, shape into 6 oval patties. Grill or broil the patties until cooked according to your preference; reserve 1 cup cooking juices for preparation of the accompanying sauce. Drizzle sauce maison on each patty and serve.

SAUCE MAISON

$\mathcal{I}$n a small skillet, cook the butter over medium heat until golden brown. Stir in the Worcestershire and meat juices and cook for 1 minute. Add the parsley and keep the sauce warm until serving.

Yields 1½ cups

¾ cup (1½ sticks) butter

---

2 tablespoons
    Worcestershire sauce

---

1 cup meat juices
    (Beef stock can be
    substituted.)

---

1 teaspoon chopped
    fresh parsley

MAUDE'S
SPAGHETTI AND MEATBALLS

8 Servings

---

2 pounds ground veal round (Ground beef round can be substituted.)

---

2 medium onions, finely chopped

---

4 celery ribs, finely chopped

---

1 small green bell pepper, finely chopped

---

10 garlic cloves, very finely chopped

---

3 tablespoons freshly grated Parmesan cheese

---

3 large eggs, well beaten

---

1 cup seasoned bread crumbs

Vegetable oil for frying

---

4 sprigs fresh parsley, finely chopped

---

1 scallion, finely chopped

---

6 ounces (³/₄ cup) tomato paste

---

*I*n a large bowl, combine the veal, half the onion, half the celery, half the bell pepper, and 4 of the chopped garlic cloves. Sprinkle in the Parmesan cheese, then add the eggs. Season with 2 teaspoons salt and at least ¾ teaspoon black pepper, then gently knead the mixture with your fingers, blending the ingredients thoroughly.

Spread the bread crumbs on a plate. Form about ¼ cup of the meat mixture into a ball, roll the ball in the bread crumbs, then set it on a clean tray or platter. Follow the same procedure with the remainder of the meat mixture.

Pour vegetable oil to a depth of ½-inch into a large, deep skillet. Heat the oil over moderately high heat to a temperature of about 340 degrees F. Fry the meatballs, in batches, in the hot oil until brown on all sides. Remove the cooked meatballs from the pan with a slotted spoon and set aside. Reserve the pan drippings.

To make the tomato sauce, sauté the remaining onion, celery, bell pepper, parsley, and scallions in the meatball pan drippings. Cook the vegetables a few minutes, then stir in the tomato paste. Simmer another 2 minutes, then add the sugar, tomato sauce, 2⅓ cups water, and the bay leaves. Season the sauce with at least 1½ teaspoons salt and ¾ teaspoon pepper. When the ingredients are well combined, place the meatballs in the sauce and cook over low heat for about 1 hour; stir gently several times during cooking, being careful not to break apart the meatballs. Remove the bay leaves before serving.

Cook the spaghetti in boiling salted water for 8 to 10 minutes, until al dente. Drain the pasta and place a portion on each plate. Top the spaghetti with about ⅔ cup sauce and 2 meatballs. Garnish with freshly grated Romano cheese.

¼	*teaspoon sugar*
16	*ounces (2 cups) tomato sauce*
2⅓	*cups water*
2	*bay leaves, crushed*
	Salt and black pepper
2	*pounds spaghetti*
	Freshly grated Romano cheese for garnish

TOURNEDOS CHANTECLAIR

4 Servings

12	beef tournedos, about 3 ounces each
2	tablespoons butter
¼	cup béarnaise sauce (see Index)
¼	cup marchand de vin sauce (see Index)
¼	cup choron sauce (recipe follows)

elt the butter in a large sauté pan and cook

the tournedos over moderately high heat until done according

to preference.

Serve each person 3 tournedos topped with a different sauce.

CHORON SAUCE

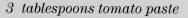

3	tablespoons tomato paste
1	cup béarnaise sauce (see Index)
1	tablespoon red wine

ombine the ingredients in a small bowl and stir until

well blended.

TOURNEDOS LESLIE

4 Servings

16 carrot sticks

16 marinated baby corn

8 broccoli florets

8 cauliflower florets

¼ cup (½ stick) butter

8 beef tournedos, 2 to 3
     ounces each

All-purpose flour for dusting

¼ cup beef stock (see Index)

2 teaspoons green
    peppercorns

¾ cup port wine

4 ounces goat cheese

salt and black pepper

*B*lanch the carrot, baby corn, broccoli, and cauliflower for 4 minutes in boiling water. Melt 2 tablespoons of the butter in a medium skillet and quickly stir-fry the vegetables.

Season the beef with salt and pepper, then dust lightly with flour. Melt the remaining 2 tablespoons butter in a large sauté pan and cook the meat over medium heat about 1½ minutes per side or until done to preference.

Remove the filets from the pan and set aside. Drain the excess butter from the pan and add the stock and green peppercorns.

Reduce the mixture over moderately high heat about 1 minute, then add the port and reduce another 2 minutes.

Preheat a broiler.

Place 2 tournedos on ovenproof plates and top each with ½ ounce of goat cheese. Drizzle the reduced stock over the cheese, then garnish the plates with stir-fried vegetables. Place the plates under the broiler for 1 minute to soften the goat cheese. Serve immediately.

TOURNEDOS ROYAL WITH SWEETBREADS

4 Servings

4 artichokes
12 ounces sweetbreads
¼ cup (½ stick) butter
½ cup chopped onion
¼ cup seasoned bread crumbs
1 teaspoon paprika
1 teaspoon capers
1 teaspoon chopped truffles
Pinch of thyme leaves
¼ cup béarnaise sauce (see Index)
4 filets mignons, 12 to 14 ounces each
Salt and black pepper

Trim the stems and leaves from the artichokes and boil the bottoms for 20 to 30 minutes until tender. Remove the furry choke and set the artichoke bottoms aside.

Rinse the sweetbreads, then cook them in boiling salted water for 5 to 7 minutes. Drain and finely chop the sweetbreads.

Preheat oven to 350 degrees F.

Melt the butter in a small skillet and sauté the onion until tender. Reduce the heat to medium and add the bread crumbs, paprika, capers, truffles, thyme, and sweetbreads. Cook the mixture until heated through, then remove from the heat and divide into 4 parts. Roll each part into a ball and place in an artichoke bottom. Set the artichoke bottoms on a lightly oiled baking sheet and place in the hot oven while preparing the filets mignons.

Preheat a grill or broiler.

Season the steaks with salt and pepper, then grill or broil until done to preference.

Place a filet mignon on each plate and top with 1 tablespoon of béarnaise sauce. Set a stuffed artichoke bottom on the side of the meat and serve.

CRÉOLE JAMBALAYA

Melt the butter in a large saucepan or Dutch oven, and add the scallions, bell pepper, celery, and garlic. Sauté the vegetables until tender, then add the shrimp and oysters. Cook the mixture another 5 minutes, then add the remaining ingredients, except the rice. Reduce the heat and simmer for 10 to 15 minutes. Stir in the rice and cover the pan. Cook the jambalaya for 25 to 30 minutes until the rice is tender.

4 Servings

⅓	cup butter
½	cup chopped scallions
⅓	cup chopped green bell pepper
½	cup chopped celery
1	tablespoon minced garlic
8	ounces medium shrimp, peeled and deveined
24	shucked oysters
2	cups fresh or canned tomatoes
1	cup water
1	bay leaf
½	teaspoon salt
¼	teaspoon cayenne pepper
1	cup raw white rice, rinsed

STUFFED BELL PEPPER
PLAQUEMINES

4 Servings

4 large green bell peppers
2 quarts water
½ cup (1 stick) butter
½ cup onion, finely chopped
1 pound lean ground beef
3 garlic cloves, finely chopped
½ cup chopped scallions
1 teaspoon Italian seasoning
¼ cup beef stock (see Index)
3 ripe tomatoes, chopped
1 cup white rice (see Index)
1 tablespoon chopped fresh parsley
2 large eggs
2 tablespoons freshly grated Parmesan cheese
2 tablespoons seasoned bread crumbs
Salt and black pepper

*S*lice off the tops of the bell peppers and remove the seeds from inside.

Bring 2 quarts of water to a boil in a large pot. Drop the peppers into the water and blanch for 5 to 6 minutes. Remove the peppers from the pot and drain.

Preheat oven to 350 degrees F.

Melt the butter in a large skillet and sauté the onion, ground beef, and garlic; cook the mixture for 5 to 10 minutes over medium heat until the meat browns. Add the scallions, Italian seasoning, stock, and tomatoes. Mix well and season to taste with salt and pepper. Fold the rice into the mixture, then add the parsley and eggs.

Fill the bell peppers with the beef mixture and sprinkle Parmesan cheese and bread crumbs on top; reserve the remaining beef filling for presentation. Place the peppers upright on a baking sheet and bake in the hot oven about 5 minutes.

Divide the remaining beef filling between four plates, set a stuffed pepper in the center of each bed of filling, and serve.

OLD N'AWLINS STUFFED CABBAGE CRÉOLE

Melt 1 tablespoon of the butter in a large skillet and brown the ground beef. Fold in the shrimp and tomatoes; cook, stirring, until the shrimp turn pink, then add 1½ cups of the Créole sauce. Simmer the mixture for 10 minutes, then stir in the white rice. Set the filling aside while preparing the cabbage.

Fill a large pot with water and add the remaining ¼ cup butter. Bring the buttered water to a boil. Core the cabbage and drop the head into the boiling water. Cook the cabbage about 20 minutes until the leaves become limp and begin to separate.

Remove the cabbage from the pot and drain. When cool enough to handle, peel off 8 large leaves. Place a generous portion of the beef and shrimp filling on the base of each leaf, then roll the leaves, tucking in the sides. Place the cabbage rolls in a shallow baking dish.

Preheat oven to 350 degrees F.

Chop the leftover cabbage and combine it with the remaining 1½ cups Créole sauce. Pour the cabbage and Créole sauce mixture over the stuffed cabbage, then sprinkle with bread crumbs. Bake in the hot oven for 20 to 25 minutes and serve.

8 Servings

¼	cup (½ stick) plus 1 tablespoon butter
1	pound lean ground beef
2	pounds medium shrimp, peeled and deveined
1½	pounds (about 5 medium) tomatoes, chopped
3	cups Créole sauce (see Index)
2	cups white rice (see Index)
1	large head of cabbage
¾	cup seasoned bread crumbs

Stuffed Eggplant Dauphine

4 Servings

---

2 eggplants, about 1 pound
   each

---

2 tablespoons olive oil

---

1 shallot, minced

---

4 small tomatoes, peeled,
   seeded and diced

---

1 teaspoon minced fresh
   oregano leaves

1¼ teaspoons minced fresh
    basil leaves

1¼ teaspoons minced fresh
    thyme leaves

1½ cups chicken stock
    (see Index)

---

1 bay leaf

---

1 pound lump crabmeat,
   picked over to remove
   any shell and cartilage

---

1 teaspoon chopped garlic

---

4 ounces (½ cup) peeled
   and deveined medium
   shrimp, diced

---

2 tablespoons chopped
   fresh parsley

1¼ cups seasoned bread
    crumbs

½ cup freshly grated
   Parmesan cheese

---

*S*plit the eggplants in half lengthwise and scoop out the pulp, being careful not to tear the skin. Chop the eggplant pulp and set it aside.

Heat the olive oil in a large saucepan or Dutch oven and sauté the shallot until tender. Add the tomatoes, oregano, basil, thyme, and eggplant pulp and stir until well combined. Place the remaining ingredients, through the parsley, in the pan, and mix well. Fold in 1 cup of the bread crumbs and cook the stuffing for 3 to 5 minutes over medium heat; remove the bay leaf.

Preheat oven to 375 degrees F.

Fill the eggplant shells with the stuffing and sprinkle with the remaining bread crumbs and the Parmesan cheese. Place the eggplants on a lightly oiled baking sheet and bake in the hot oven for 20 to 25 minutes until hot.

STUFFED SUMMER SQUASH
AU GRATIN

8 Servings

*C*ut a slice from the squash lengthwise and scoop out the pulp. Dice the pulp and set aside.

Blanch the carrot in boiling water for 1½ minutes, then drain. Melt the butter in a large skillet and sauté the salmon and shrimp for 1 minute, then blend in the flour. Add the scallops, zucchini, squash pulp, and diced carrot. Cook the mixture about 15 minutes over medium heat, then stir in the cream, oysters, and crabmeat.

Preheat oven to 350 degrees F.

Fill the squash skins with the crabmeat stuffing and transfer to an oiled baking sheet. Sprinkle the stuffed squash with the Romano and Parmesan cheeses and with bread crumbs. Bake in the hot oven for 20 to 30 minutes and serve. Any leftover stuffing can be baked in a small dish.

8	*large yellow squash*
1	*large carrot, diced (about 1½ cups)*
8	*ounces salmon fillets, cubed*
8	*ounces peeled and deveined small shrimp*
1	*tablespoon all-purpose flour*
16	*small bay scallops*
1	*large zuchhini, diced*
1	*cup heavy cream*
16	*poached oysters*
8	*ounces lump crabmeat, picked over to remove any shell and cartilage*
½	*cup freshly grated Romano cheese*
½	*cup freshly grated Parmesan cheese*
2	*teaspoons seasoned bread crumbs*

Salt and white pepper

3 small loaves French bread
(approximately
12 inches in length)

½ cup garlic butter
(see Index)

2 tablespoons paprika

3 tablespoons fresh
parsley, finely chopped

½ cup freshly grated
Parmesan cheese

Preheat oven to 350 degrees F.

GARLIC BREAD

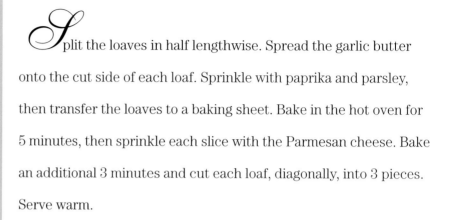

*S*plit the loaves in half lengthwise. Spread the garlic butter

onto the cut side of each loaf. Sprinkle with paprika and parsley,

then transfer the loaves to a baking sheet. Bake in the hot oven for

5 minutes, then sprinkle each slice with the Parmesan cheese. Bake

an additional 3 minutes and cut each loaf, diagonally, into 3 pieces.

Serve warm.

> *"Do you like garlic bread? Then here's the perfect answer to how to make it.
> Owen Brennan, vigorous, imaginative, one of New Orleans' first citizens,
> gave us the directions as he sat at our table in his softly lighted, quiet French
> and Créole restaurant."*
>
> Gaynor Maddox
> Plattsburgh Press-Republican
> Plattsburgh, New York
> January 11, 1953

6 Servings

¼ cup (½ stick) butter

2 small loaves
French bread,
(approximately
12 inches in length)
split lengthwise

1 teaspoon cinnamon

1 teaspoon sugar

CINNAMON TOAST

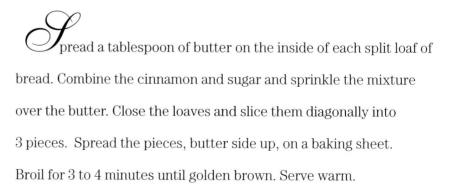

*S*pread a tablespoon of butter on the inside of each split loaf of

bread. Combine the cinnamon and sugar and sprinkle the mixture

over the butter. Close the loaves and slice them diagonally into

3 pieces. Spread the pieces, butter side up, on a baking sheet.

Broil for 3 to 4 minutes until golden brown. Serve warm.

Glazed Carrots

4 Servings

4 carrots

½ cup (1 stick) butter

½ cup sugar

1 cup water

*P*eel the carrots and slice them into rings, about ⅛-inch thick. Combine the butter and sugar in a large saucepan, along with 1 cup of water. Add the carrots, then bring the mixture to a boil. Reduce the heat, cover the pan and cook the carrots until tender, about 15 minutes.

Plantation Grits

8 to 10 Servings

5 cups water

1 teaspoon salt

1 cup grits

¼ cup (½ stick butter)

*I*n a medium saucepan, bring 5 cups of water to a boil along with the salt. Gradually add the grits to the pan, stirring constantly. Reduce the heat and simmer the grits until thickened, 5 to 10 minutes. Add the butter and stir until the butter is melted throughout.

OYSTER DRESSING

Yields 3 cups

½ cup (1 stick) butter
½ cup onion, finely chopped
½ cup celery, finely chopped
½ cup green bell pepper, finely chopped
2 tablespoons minced garlic
1 large bay leaf
Pinch of thyme
1 tablespoon Worcestershire sauce
24 shucked oysters
1 large egg
2 cups seasoned bread crumbs
1 tablespoon parsley, finely chopped
Salt and black pepper

*M*elt the butter in a large skillet and sauté the onion, celery, bell pepper, and garlic. When the vegetables are tender, add the bay leaf, thyme, Worcestershire, and oysters, along with any oyster water. Cook for 2 to 3 minutes, until the edges of the oysters begin to curl. Season the mixture with salt and pepper to taste, then working quickly, stir in the egg. Fold in the bread crumbs and parsley and cook for 1 to 2 minutes longer until the mixture is heated through. Refrigerate until use.

Brennan's
Au Gratin Potatoes

❧

6 to 8 Servings

By hand or using a mandoline, cut the potatoes into slices about ⅛-inch thick. Bring 6 cups of water to a boil in a large saucepan; drop the potato slices into the water and boil for about 5 minutes. Pour the potatoes into a colander and let drain.

Preheat oven to 375 degrees F.

Place the cream in a saucepan and reduce over moderately high heat about 15 minutes until thickened, whisking frequently. Add the white pepper and about ¾ cup of each cheese. Whisk constantly until the cheese melts, then add the wine and potato slices. Cook the mixture another 5 minutes on top of the stove, then transfer it to a baking dish. Sprinkle with the remaining cheeses and set the dish in a larger baking dish or pan filled with about a half inch of water. Bake the potatoes in the water bath for 15 minutes, then broil for 3 to 5 minutes until golden brown. Serve immediately.

4	*large Idaho potatoes, peeled*
6	*cups water*
3	*cups heavy cream*
¼	*teaspoon white pepper*
1	*cup freshly shredded Parmesan cheese*
1	*cup freshly shredded Romano cheese*
2	*tablespoons dry white wine*

BERNY POTATOES

8 Servings

3 Idaho potatoes, peeled and cubed
½ cup milk
1 cup ham, finely chopped
1 cup scallions, finely chopped
2 egg yolks
1 cup grated almonds
Salt and white pepper
Oil for deep frying

*P*lace the potatoes in a large saucepan and cover with cold water. Add ½ teaspoon salt and boil the potatoes until very tender, 15 to 20 minutes. Drain the potatoes and mash them by hand or using an electric mixer. Set the mashed potatoes aside.

Combine the milk, ham, and scallions in a large sauté pan and bring the mixture to a boil. Stir in the mashed potatoes, then season to taste with salt and pepper. Beat in the egg yolks, then form the potato mixture into balls about 2 inches in diameter. Roll the balls in the almonds, making about 16 in all. Heat oil in a deep fryer to 350 degrees F. Fry the potato balls in batches about 5 minutes until golden brown. Blot on paper towels, then serve.

BRABANT POTATOES

Place the potatoes in a large saucepan and add water to cover; boil the potatoes until tender, about 15 to 20 minutes. Drain the potatoes and set aside.

Melt the butter in a large skillet and cook the garlic a few minutes over medium heat. Add the potatoes, paprika, salt, and parsley. Cook briefly, stirring, until the potatoes are well coated with the seasonings. Serve hot.

4 Servings

2	*large Idaho potatoes, peeled and cubed*
¼	*cup (½ stick) butter*
1	*tablespoon minced garlic*

Pinch of paprika

Pinch of salt

1	*tablespoon chopped fresh parsley*

MASHED POTATOES RANDOLPH

8 Servings

3½	cups water
4	medium potatoes, peeled and sliced
2	cups milk
¼	cup (½ stick) butter
1	cup heavy cream
Salt and white pepper	

*B*ring 3½ cups water to a boil in a large saucepan, then add the potatoes and milk. Cook the potatoes over medium high heat for 25 minutes until very tender.

Drain the potatoes and whip with an electric mixer until lump free. Add the butter and heavy cream, then season with salt and pepper to taste.

STUFFED BAKED POTATOES

Bake the potatoes in the hot oven for 1 hour until tender. Remove the potatoes from the oven and let cool.

Reduce the oven temperature to 350 degrees F.

In a medium skillet, fry the bacon until crisp. Lift the strips out of the pan with a slotted spoon and drain all but 2 tablespoons of the drippings from the pan. Crumble the bacon and set it aside.

Sauté the scallions in the pan drippings for several minutes until tender. When the onion is cooked, remove the pan from the heat.

Make a shallow slit in the potatoes, lengthwise, being careful not to cut all the way through the potato. Scoop out the pulp from the potatoes; combine the pulp with the scallions and set the potato skins aside. Blend the Parmesan, sour cream, and crumbled bacon into the potato and scallion mixture, mashing the potato as the ingredients are combined. Season with salt and pepper to taste, then place the skillet over low heat to warm the potato mixture.

Spoon the mashed potato into the potato skins, drizzle with melted butter, and sprinkle with paprika. Bake in the hot oven for 15 to 20 minutes, then serve.

4 Servings

4 large Idaho potatoes, jackets scrubbed

8 strips of bacon

½ cup chopped scallions

¼ cup freshly grated Parmesan cheese

1 cup sour cream

2 tablespoons melted butter

Dash of paprika

Salt and black pepper

Preheat oven to 400 degrees F.

SIDE DISHES   239

SWEET POTATOES

4 Servings

4	medium sweet potatoes
¼	cup melted butter plus extra for brushing
¼	cup chopped pecans
¼	cup raisins (optional)
½	cup heavy cream
¼	teaspoon nutmeg
¼	teaspoon cinnamon
¾	cup miniature marshmallows
2	tablespoons sugar

Preheat oven to 350 degrees F.

*B*rush the sweet potatoes with melted butter and place them on a baking sheet. Bake in the hot oven until tender, about 1 hour.

Remove the sweet potatoes from the oven; when cool enough to handle, slice a wedge from each potato, so that their shape resembles a horn or cornucopia. Scoop out the pulp from each sweet potato horn, and place the pulp in a bowl with ¼ cup melted butter. Reserve the sweet potato skins.

Mash the sweet potato pulp, then add the remaining ingredients. Spoon or pipe the pulp mixture into the sweet potato skins and place them on a baking sheet. Sprinkle the sweet potatoes with sugar and bake in the hot oven for 5 minutes. Serve hot.

BAKED MACARONI ANNIE

Bring 2 quarts of water to a boil. Add the macaroni and cook, stirring frequently, 7 to 10 minutes until tender. Drain the macaroni in a colander.

In a large mixing bowl, beat the eggs slightly, then add the cream. Season the mixture with salt and pepper to taste. Stir in the cheese, then add the macaroni and toss.

Slice the butter and place the pats in the bottom of a 13 x 9 x 2-inch baking dish. Pour the macaroni into the baking dish and, if desired, top with slices of cheese. Place the baking dish in a larger pan containing ½-inch of water and bake until set and lightly browned, 35 to 45 minutes.

8 to 10 Servings

2 quarts water

1 pound #1 elbow macaroni

12 eggs

2 cups heavy cream or Pet® milk

Salt and white pepper

1 pound sharp cheddar cheese, cubed (plus extra sliced cheddar for the top of the casserole, if desired)

½ cup (1 stick) butter

Preheat oven to 400 degrees F.

CREAMED SPINACH

Yields 3 cups

¾ cup (1½ sticks) butter

---

10 ounces fresh spinach
     leaves, washed,
     stemmed and chopped

1½ cups onion,
     finely chopped

¼ cup all-purpose flour

---

2 cups scalded milk

---

1 teaspoon salt

Pinch of white pepper

Pinch of nutmeg

---

*M*elt ½ cup butter in a large sauté pan; add the spinach and cook over medium heat a few minutes until wilted.

In a large saucepan, melt the remaining ¼ cup butter. Add the onion and cook over medium heat until tender. Using a whisk, blend the flour into the mixture, then gradually pour in the milk. Stir until smooth, then add the spinach. Season with salt, white pepper, and nutmeg. When the mixture is thick and warmed through, remove it from the heat and serve.

GRILLED TOMATOES

✥

4 Servings

Cut a thin slice off the stem and base ends of the tomatoes, then slice them in half crosswise. Bake on a greased baking sheet or grill the tomatoes until soft. Sprinkle with Parmesan cheese, then broil until the cheese melts.

2 large ripe tomatoes

½ cup freshly grated
     Parmesan cheese

Preheat oven to 375 degrees F. or light a grill.

WHITE RICE

✥

4 Servings

Place the rice in a saucepan and add 2 cups of water. Bring the mixture to a boil over high heat. Stir the rice, then reduce the heat to low and cover the pan. Simmer for 20 minutes, remove the pan from the heat and let the rice sit, covered, for a few minutes in the pan. Just before serving, fluff the rice with a fork and season with salt and pepper to taste.

1 cup long grain rice

2 cups water

Salt and black pepper

$\mathcal{D}$ESSERTS

APPLE TART BARRETT

6 Servings

3 large apples, peeled and cored
3 tablespoons water
3 tablespoons lemon juice
3 tablespoons apple schnapps
3 tablespoons ginger liqueur
1 cup sugar plus extra for sprinkling
10 black peppercorns
8 cloves
¼ cup raisins
¼ cup chopped pecans
One 14 x 11-inch sheet of puff pastry
1 large egg
¼ cup milk
¼ cup (½ stick) butter

Cut the apples into very thin slices and place in a large mixing bowl with 3 tablespoons water. Add the remaining ingredients, through the pecans, then toss until the apples are well coated. Cover the bowl and marinate the apples for 2 hours in the refrigerator.

While the apples are marinating, prepare the tart shells. Line a baking sheet with parchment paper and set aside. In a small bowl, beat the egg with the milk. Spread the sheet of puff pastry on a floured work surface, brush with the egg wash, and cut into six 3 x 5-inch rectangles, twenty-four 5 x ¼-inch strips, and twenty-four 3 x ¼-inch strips. Transfer the pastry rectangles to the prepared baking sheet and layer two thicknesses of the pastry strips on all four sides of the rectangle to form a shallow box. Make six boxes in all.

Preheat oven to 375 degrees F.

Remove the apples from the refrigerator and transfer to a medium saucepan. Bring the mixture to a boil and cook for 15 minutes, then strain the apples and other solid ingredients from the liquid. Fill the pastry boxes with the apple mixture.

Reduce the marinating liquid over high heat until thickened, about 15 to 20 minutes, then drizzle over the tarts. Sprinkle the tarts with sugar and dot each with 2 teaspoons butter. Bake the pastry in the hot oven until it puffs and browns, about 20 to 25 minutes.
Serve warm.

BANANAS FOSTER

4 Servings

¼	cup (½ stick) butter
1	cup brown sugar
½	teaspoon cinnamon
¼	cup banana liqueur
4	bananas, cut in half lengthwise, then halved
¼	cup dark rum
4	scoops vanilla ice cream

Combine the butter, sugar, and cinnamon in a flambé pan or skillet. Place the pan over low heat either on an alcohol burner or on top of the stove, and cook, stirring, until the sugar dissolves. Stir in the banana liqueur, then place the bananas in the pan. When the banana sections soften and begin to brown, carefully add the rum. Continue to cook the sauce until the rum is hot, then tip the pan slightly to ignite the rum. When the flames subside, lift the bananas out of the pan and place four pieces over each portion of ice cream. Generously spoon warm sauce over the top of the ice cream and serve immediately.

In the 1950's, New Orleans was the major port of entry for bananas shipped from Central and South America. Owen Edward Brennan challenged his talented chef, Paul Blangé, to include bananas in a new culinary creation – Owen's way of promoting the imported fruit. Simultaneously, Holiday Magazine *had asked Owen to provide a new recipe to appear in a feature article on Brennan's.*

In 1951, Chef Paul created Bananas Foster. The scrumptious dessert was named for Richard Foster, who, as chairman, served with Owen on the New Orleans Crime Commission, a civic effort to clean up the French Quarter. Richard Foster, owner of the Foster Awning Company, was a frequent customer of Brennan's and a very good friend of Owen.

Little did anyone realize that Bananas Foster would become an international favorite and is the most requested item on the restaurant's menu. Thirty-five thousand pounds of bananas are flamed each year at Brennan's in the preparation of its world-famous dessert.

BEIGNETS MARDI GRAS

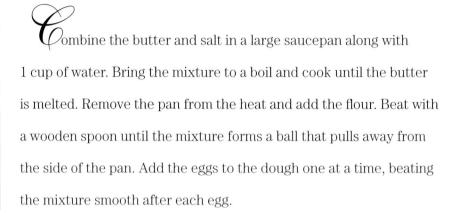

Yields 24 beignets

½ *cup (1 stick) butter*

Pinch of salt

---

1 *cup water*

---

1 *cup all-purpose flour*

---

4 *large eggs*

---

1 *tablespoon sugar*

½ *teaspoon grated
orange peel*

½ *teaspoon grated
lemon peel*

Oil for deep frying

Powdered sugar for dusting

Whiskey Sauce (see Index)

---

*Strawberry sauce, optional
(recipe follows)*

---

*C*ombine the butter and salt in a large saucepan along with 1 cup of water. Bring the mixture to a boil and cook until the butter is melted. Remove the pan from the heat and add the flour. Beat with a wooden spoon until the mixture forms a ball that pulls away from the side of the pan. Add the eggs to the dough one at a time, beating the mixture smooth after each egg.

Stir in the sugar and citrus peel, then drop the dough by heaping teaspoons into oil heated in a deep fryer to 350 degrees F. Fry the beignets in batches, gently turning them, until golden brown and cooked through, about 10 to 12 minutes. Drain on paper towels and dust with powdered sugar.

Serve the warm beignets in pools of room temperature whiskey sauce (see Index). Strawberry sauce can be substituted.

STRAWBERRY SAUCE

Heat the sugar briefly in a large saucepan over low heat, then add the remaining ingredients. Increase the heat to medium and cook, stirring, until the mixture reaches a low boil. Cook for 5 minutes, then remove the mixture from the heat and strain in a fine sieve. Serve the strawberry sauce either at room temperature or chilled.

Yields 2½ cups

¼	cup powdered sugar
1	quart (4 cups) fresh strawberries
1	cup jellied cranberry sauce
1	tablespoon strawberry liqueur
¼	teaspoon grated lemon peel
¼	teaspoon grated orange peel

BREAD PUDDING AND WHISKEY SAUCE

❧

15 to 18 Servings

½	cup raisins
4	cups milk
1	cup heavy cream
4	large eggs
1½	cups sugar
½	cup chopped pecans
1	teaspoon cinnamon
1	teaspoon nutmeg
1	teaspoon vanilla
1	stale loaf French bread, about 14 ounces
6	tablespoons butter plus extra for buttering baking dish

Whiskey sauce (recipe follows)

Preheat oven to 350 degrees F.

*P*lace the raisins in a small bowl and add warm water to cover. Soak for 2 hours, then drain.

In a large mixing bowl, combine the milk, cream, eggs, sugar, raisins, and pecans. Whisk the mixture until well blended, then stir in the cinnamon, nutmeg, and vanilla. Break the bread into the bowl and fold the mixture until the bread is soggy.

Butter a large loaf pan or 13 x 9 x 2-inch baking dish and pour in the bread mixture. Push 6 tablespoons of butter into the top of the loaf and set the pan in a larger pan filled with about ½-inch of water. Bake the bread pudding in the water bath for 30 minutes, then remove the larger pan from the oven; bake the bread pudding for another 45 minutes.

Slice the bread pudding and serve warm topped with whiskey sauce.

WHISKEY SAUCE

Yields 1 cup

3	*large eggs*
1	*cup sugar*
1	*teaspoon vanilla*
½	*cup milk*
1	*tablespoon cornstarch*
¼	*cup cold water*
3	*tablespoons* *Canadian whiskey*

*P*lace the eggs in a large saucepan and whisk over medium heat until slightly thickened. Add the sugar, vanilla, and milk and cook until hot; do not let the mixture come to a boil.

In a small bowl, blend the cornstarch into ¼ cup cold water. Stir the cornstarch into the egg mixture, stirring constantly. Add the whiskey and cook the sauce over medium heat until smooth and thick enough to coat the back of a spoon, about 15 minutes; stir frequently.

Serve the whiskey sauce either at room temperature, or chill and serve cold.

CRÊPES

Yields 16 crêpes

---

3 *large eggs*

1 *cup milk*

½ *cup all-purpose flour*

Melted butter for brushing

$\mathscr{I}$n a medium bowl, beat the eggs with the milk. Add the flour and whisk until smooth. Strain the batter to remove any lumps.

Preheat a 5-inch crêpe pan or skillet, and brush it lightly with melted butter. Pour about 2 tablespoons batter into the pan and tilt the pan to spread the batter evenly over the bottom of the pan. Cook the crêpe over medium heat until golden brown, about 30 seconds, then turn the crêpe and brown the other side.

Repeat the procedure with the remaining batter, making about 16 crêpes in all. The crêpes can be sealed in plastic wrap and frozen for several weeks.

CRÊPES BRIDGET

In a mixing bowl, combine the cream cheese, sour cream, sugar, and vanilla. Beat the mixture until smooth. Place 3 tablespoons of the cream cheese filling on one end of each crêpe; roll the crêpes, then refrigerate them until serving.

Spread the almonds on a baking sheet and toast in a preheated 300 degrees F. oven for 5 to 8 minutes. Let cool.

Stir the crème de cocoa into the warm hot fudge sauce. Place 2 crêpes on each plate and spoon the liqueur-flavored chocolate sauce over the crêpes. Top with whipped cream and toasted almonds.

8 Servings

1	pound room temperature cream cheese
5	tablespoons sour cream
2	tablespoons sugar
1	tablespoon vanilla
16	crêpes (see Index)
½	cup sliced almonds
2	cups hot fudge sauce (recipe follows)
¼	cup dark crème de cocoa
2	cups whipped cream

HOT FUDGE SAUCE

Combine the butter and chocolate in the top of a double boiler over simmering water. Cook the mixture, stirring, until the chocolate has melted, then blend in ⅔ cup boiling water. When the mixture is smooth, add the sugar and corn syrup. Place the pan over direct heat and bring the sauce to a low boil. Cover the pan and cook over medium heat for 2 to 3 minutes. Uncover the pan, reduce the heat to low, then simmer an additional 2 minutes.

Serve immediately, or cover and refrigerate. To reheat the hot fudge, warm it over low heat.

Yields 2 cups

4	ounces unsweetened chocolate
2	tablespoons butter
⅔	cup boiling water
2	cups sugar
¼	cup light corn syrup

CRÊPES FITZGERALD

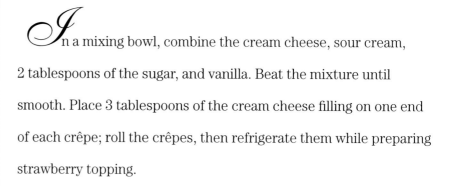

8 Servings

---

1 pound room temperature
  cream cheese

---

5 tablespoons sour cream

---

10 tablespoons sugar

---

1 tablespoon vanilla

---

16 crêpes (see Index)

---

1 tablespoon butter

---

5 cups fresh strawberries,
  stemmed and sliced

Juice of ½ lemon

---

2 tablespoons
  maraschino liqueur

---

*I*n a mixing bowl, combine the cream cheese, sour cream, 2 tablespoons of the sugar, and vanilla. Beat the mixture until smooth. Place 3 tablespoons of the cream cheese filling on one end of each crêpe; roll the crêpes, then refrigerate them while preparing strawberry topping.

Place the butter and remaining 8 tablespoons sugar in a large saucepan. Cook for several minutes over medium heat, stirring, until the sugar dissolves. Add the strawberries and lemon juice; bring the mixture to a boil over high heat, then reduce the heat to medium and cook for 10 to 12 minutes until the liquid thickens; cooking time will depend on the ripeness of the strawberries. Add the maraschino liqueur and flame the mixture.

To serve, place two crêpes on each plate and spoon about ¾ cup warm strawberry topping over the crêpes.

CRÊPES SUZETTE

*M*elt the butter in a chafing dish or skillet. Add the orange and lemon peel to the pan and cook briefly until tender. Stir in the sugar, orange juice, and lemon juice; cook the sauce, stirring, until syrupy. Place the crêpes in the sauce, three at a time. When the crêpes are coated with sauce, fold each crêpe in half and then into quarters. When all 12 crêpes have been added to the pan, pour the Cointreau, Grand Marnier, and brandy over them, then tip the pan slightly to ignite the brandy. When the flames subside, place 3 crêpes on each plate, and top with some of the sauce and citrus peel.

4 Servings

¼ cup (½ stick) butter

Peel of 2 oranges,
    thinly slivered

Peel of 1 lemon,
    thinly slivered

¼ cup sugar

Juice of ½ orange

Juice of ½ lemon

1 tablespoon Cointreau

1 tablespoon Grand Marnier

2 tablespoons brandy

12 crêpes (see Index)

CRÈME CARAMEL LOUISIANE

8 Servings

1	cup sugar
2	cans condensed milk
2	condensed milk cans of water
2	tablespoons vanilla
8	eggs

Preheat oven to 350 degrees F.

*I*n a heavy skillet melt the sugar stirring constantly until brown and syrupy. Pour into a 8 x 11$\frac{1}{2}$ x 2 inch pyrex dish to harden.

In a mixing bowl, combine the remaining ingredients. Pour into the pyrex dish and place the dish in a larger, shallow pan filled with water.

Bake the custard in its water bath for 1$\frac{1}{2}$ hours. Then test the doneness by inserting a knife in the center of the custard; if the knife comes out clean the custard is done. Cool at room temperature.

An intense and delicious Créole egg custard!

FLOATING ISLAND

※

Warm the milk in a large sauté pan to about 170 degrees F.; do not let the milk reach a boil.

Combine the egg whites and salt in a large bowl and beat to soft peaks. Add the sugar and beat until glossy and stiff. Fill a 4-ounce ice cream scoop or large spoon with meringue, rounding the top. Slide the meringue out of the scoop and into the hot milk. Poach about 4 minutes, turning the meringue balls once.

Remove the meringue balls with a slotted spoon and place on a tray lined with wax paper.

Spoon whiskey sauce onto eight plates and place a meringue "island" in the center of each plate.

8 Servings

2	*cups milk*
6	*egg whites*
$\frac{1}{4}$	*teaspoon salt*
$\frac{3}{4}$	*cup sugar*

Whiskey sauce (see Index)

Brennan's Lemon Curd Tartelette

16 Servings

¼ cup grated lemon peel

½ cup lemon juice

2 cups sugar

4 large eggs

1 cup (2 sticks) butter

1 cup heavy cream

2 tablespoons
   powdered sugar

½ teaspoon vanilla

16 small tart shells
    (recipe follows)

*I*n the top of a double boiler, combine the lemon peel, lemon juice, and sugar. Cook the mixture over simmering water until the sugar dissolves, then whisk in the eggs and butter and cook until thick enough to coat the back of a spoon, about 5 to 10 minutes. Transfer the lemon curd to a bowl and cool to room temperature, then refrigerate for 1 to 1½ hours; the curd will thicken as it chills, but not become as thick as pie filling.

In a medium bowl, whip the cream until stiff, then fold in the powdered sugar and vanilla.

Spoon 2½ tablespoons chilled curd into each tart shell and top with the whipped cream.

TART SHELLS

Yields 16 tart shells

Combine the flour and salt in a large mixing bowl and make a well in the center. Place the butter in the well and cut the butter into the flour with a fork or pastry blender until the mixture is grainy. Incorporate ¼ cup cold water, 1 tablespoon at a time, to form a smooth dough. Gather the dough into a ball and knead briefly, then let rest for 15 minutes.

Preheat oven to 400 degrees F.

Quarter the dough and on a floured work surface roll each quarter into a circle about 12 inches in diameter. Cut the circles into four 4½-inch rounds; making 16 pastry rounds in all. Fit the rounds over inverted muffin tins or custard cups and prick with a fork. Bake in the hot oven until lightly browned, about 10 minutes, then cool.

Ingredients
2 cups all-purpose flour
½ teaspoon salt
1 cup (2 sticks) soft butter
¼ cup cold water

LES PÊCHES FLAMBÉES

4 Servings

---

4 ripe peaches

All-purpose flour for dredging

Oil for deep frying

½ cup (1 stick) butter

¼ cup chopped pecans

---

4 tablespoons julienned
lemon peel

---

4 tablespoons julienned
orange peel

---

2 ounces (¼ cup)
peach brandy

---

4 scoops of vanilla
ice cream

Peel the peaches and slice them in half. Remove the pits, then dredge the peach halves in flour. Deep fry the peaches in oil heated to 375 degrees F. until golden brown, 3 to 4 minutes. Drain on paper towels.

Melt the butter in a chafing dish or skillet. Place the peach halves cut side down in the pan, then add the pecans, orange peel, and lemon peel. Cook the mixture for several minutes over medium heat, until the citrus peel is tender. Pour the peach brandy into the pan, then tip the pan to ignite the brandy. When the flames subside, place two peach halves over each scoop of vanila ice cream and top with sauce.

MAUDE'S PEANUT BUTTER ICE CREAM PIE

~

*P*lace the graham cracker crumbs in a 9-inch pie pan. Moisten the crumbs with the butter and press the mixture evenly onto the bottom and sides of the pie pan. Bake in the hot oven for 2 to 3 minutes, until set. Set aside and let cool.

In a non-metallic bowl, combine the ice cream and peanut butter; work quickly, mixing the ingredients either by hand, or using an electric mixer set on medium speed.

Pour the ice cream mixture into the graham cracker crust, smooth the top, and sprinkle with chopped nuts. Freeze the pie over night or until solid, then serve.

6 to 8 Servings

1¾	cups graham cracker crumbs
¾	cup (1½ sticks) melted butter
1	quart French vanilla ice cream, softened
1	cup crunchy peanut butter
¼	cup chopped unsalted nuts

Preheat oven to 375 degrees F.

PEARS À L'AIMÉE

4 Servings

---

1 cup all-purpose flour

2 cups powdered sugar

1 large egg

1 cup milk

4 large ripe pears, peeled

Oil for deep frying

½ cup (1 stick) butter

½ cup sugar

3 tablespoons julienned
    lemon peel

3 tablespoons julienned
    orange peel

Juice of 1 lemon

Juice of 1 orange

⅛ cup chopped pecans

¼ cup pear brandy

1 cup vanilla sauce
    (recipe follows)

Combine the flour and sugar in a shallow pan or bowl. In a separate bowl, beat the egg with the milk. Dredge the pears in the flour and sugar mixture, roll them in the egg wash, then recoat with the flour mixture. Deep fry the pears in oil heated to 375 degrees F. for about 5 to 7 minutes, until tender and golden brown.

While the pears are frying, combine the butter and sugar in a skillet and cook over low heat, stirring, until the sugar has dissolved. Stir in the lemon and orange peel, along with the juices. Simmer the sauce until it reaches the consistency of a glaze, about 3 minutes, then add the pecans. Place the fried pears upright in the pan and pour in the pear brandy. Tilt the pan slightly to ignite the brandy and flame the mixture.

Spoon a pool of vanilla sauce onto each serving plate. Stand a pear in the center of the plate and arrange some of the citrus peel around the base of the pear. Pour the pecan glaze over the pear and serve.

Vanilla Sauce

Combine the ingredients in a large saucepan and bring the sauce to a low boil. Lower the heat and simmer about 15 minutes until thick enough to coat the back of a spoon. Chill before serving.

Yields 3 cups

3¼	cups heavy cream
1	cup powdered sugar
2	vanilla beans
1	teaspoon vanilla

Praline Parfait

Blend the corn syrup, pecans, walnuts, and vanilla in a small bowl to make a praline sauce. Fill four stemmed glasses with praline sauce and ice cream, layering the two ingredients. Finish with praline sauce and serve. Top with whipped cream and chopped pecans or with fresh fruit if desired.

4 Servings

1	cup dark corn syrup
½	cup chopped pecans
½	cup chopped walnuts
1	teaspoon vanilla
2	pints French vanilla ice cream

RUM CAKE MORPHY

✤

4 Servings

¼ cup (½ stick) butter

---

1 pint strawberries,
    stemmed and chopped

½ cup cabernet wine

---

4 ounces softened
    cream cheese

---

2 tablespoons heavy cream

---

1 cup plus 2 tablespoons
    powdered sugar

---

1 teaspoon vanilla

½ cup grated
    white chocolate

---

4 small rum cakes

---

2 tablespoons rum

---

*M*elt 2 tablespoons of the butter in a medium saucepan. Add the strawberries and wine to the pan, then cook the mixture about 15 minutes over medium heat until the strawberries are very tender. Push the strawberry mixture through a fine sieve. Chill the strained sauce before serving.

In a mixing bowl, beat the cream cheese until smooth, then add the heavy cream and beat until fluffy. Gradually beat in 1 cup powdered sugar, then fold in the vanilla and grated white chocolate. Fill a pastry bag fitted with a large fluted tip with the white chocolate mixture and set aside.

Combine the remaining 2 tablespoons butter and 2 tablespoons powdered sugar in a large sauté pan. When the sugar has dissolved, place the rum cakes in the pan. Add the rum to the pan and flame the rum cakes. Spoon strawberry sauce onto the base of four plates. Remove the rum cakes from the pan and gently slice them in half, horizontally. Place the bottoms of the rum cakes on the plates. Pipe some of the white chocolate mixture onto the cakes, then set the tops of the rum cakes on the filling. Pipe additional white chocolate filling on top of the rum cakes and serve.

STRAWBERRIES ROMANOFF

⚜

*I*n a large bowl, combine the strawberries, Grand Marnier, Drambuie, sugar, orange peel, and lemon peel. Cover the bowl and marinate the strawberries for 6 hours in the refrigerator.

In another bowl, beat the cream until stiff, then fold in the powdered sugar and vanilla.

Drain the strawberries and place them in a non-metallic bowl; reserve the liquid. Mash the strawberries with a fork, then fold in the ice cream. Spoon the strawberry and ice cream mixture into stemmed glasses and spoon some of the marinade over the mixture. Top with whipped cream and serve.

8 Servings

3	cups sliced strawberries
½	cup Grand Marnier
2	tablespoons Drambuie
¼	cup sugar
1	teaspoon grated orange peel
1	teaspoon grated lemon peel
1	cup heavy cream
2	tablespoons powdered sugar
1	teaspoon vanilla
2½	pints French vanilla ice cream

ABSINTHE FRAPPÉ

1 Serving

¾ *cup crushed ice*

1½ *ounces Pernod or
    Herbsaint*

---

lace the ice in a frosted old-fashioned glass. Pour the Pernod

over the ice and stir gently.

> *"An Absinthe Frappé is more costly, but far more powerful. You get the
> best one at Owen Brennan's Old Absinthe House on Bourbon Street
> in the French Quarter. The house was built in 1798 and it used to be
> one of the pirate Lafitte's favorite hangouts because of its secret
> mezzanine floor. Owen is a cheerful fellow who uses Texas Guinan's
> tactics by sometimes calling out loud to his bartender when
> strangers arrive. 'Tourist prices, Al, they look like sight-seers!'
> Then he frequently joins them and orders a round on the house."*
>   *Evans Rodger*
>   *The Baltimore Evening Sun*
>   *October 4, 1945*

ABSINTHE SUISSESSE

1 Serving

½ *ounce Pernod or
    Herbsaint*

¾ *ounce orgeat*

---

1 *egg white*

½ *cup half and half*

---

ombine all of the ingredients in a blender. Blend for

15 seconds, then pour into a frosted old-fashioned glass.

CRÉOLE BLOODY MARY

❧

Place the ice in an old-fashioned glass, then add the remaining ingredients, through the black pepper. Stir well, then squeeze the lime into the glass. Garnish with a spiced green bean and serve.

1 Serving

³/₄	cup ice cubes
1¹/₂	ounces vodka
¹/₂	teaspoon lemon juice
¹/₄	teaspoon celery salt
2	drops Tabasco®
¹/₂	cup tomato juice
1	teaspoon Worcestershire sauce

Pinch of black pepper

A wedge of lime

A spiced green-bean for garnish

BULL SHOT

❧

Place the ice cubes in a chilled old-fashioned glass. Add the remaining ingredients, except the lime, and stir well. Squeeze the lime into the glass and serve.

1 Serving

³/₄	cup ice cubes
1¹/₂	ounces vodka
3	dashes Worcestershire sauce
¹/₃	cup beef bouillon

Dash of Tabasco®

A wedge of lime for garnish

BLOODY BULL

❧

1 Serving

¾	cup ice cubes
1½	ounces vodka
½	cup tomato juice
1½	teaspoons Worcestershire sauce
¼	teaspoon celery salt
½	teaspoon lemon juice
2	drops Tabasco®
Pinch of black pepper	
1	tablespoon beef bouillon
A twist of lime peel or spiced green bean for garnish	

*P*lace the ice in an old-fashioned glass, then add the remaining ingredients through the beef bouillon. Stir and serve with a twist of lime or spiced green bean.

BRENNAN'S BRANDY MILK PUNCH

❧

1 Serving

1	cup ice cubes
1½	ounces Napoleon brandy or bourbon
2	tablespoons simple syrup (see Index)
½	cup half and half
¾	teaspoon vanilla
Pinch of nutmeg	

*C*ombine all of the ingredients, except the nutmeg, in a cocktail shaker. Shake vigorously, then pour into a chilled old-fashioned glass. Sprinkle with nutmeg and serve.

KIR

1 Serving

6 ounces dry white wine
¼ ounce crème de cassis
A twist of lemon peel for garnish

$\mathcal{P}$our the wine into a stemmed glass, then add the crème de cassis. Garnish with a lemon twist.

KIR ROYALE

1 Serving

6 ounces champagne
¼ ounce crème de cassis
A twist of lemon peel for garnish

$\mathcal{P}$our the champagne into a champagne flute, then add the crème de cassis. Garnish with a lemon twist.

MIMOSA

1 Serving

3	ounces champagne
3	ounces orange juice
1	whole ripe strawberry
1	orange slice

*P*our the champagne into a stemmed glass, then add the orange juice. Drop a strawberry into the glass and decorate the rim with a slice of orange.

MR. FUNK OF NEW ORLEANS

1 Serving

3	ounces champagne
2½	ounces cranberry juice
½	ounce peach schnapps
1	whole ripe strawberry

*P*our the champagne into a stemmed glass, then add the cranberry juice and schnapps. Garnish with a strawberry and serve.

Mr. Funk of New Orleans was created in memory of our late Cellar Master, Herman Funk.

PIRATE'S DREAM

Crush the mint sprigs in a glass large enough to hold 28 ounces of liquid. Pour in the rum, then add the grenadine, orange juice, lemon juice, and bitters. Stir well, blending the mint into the other ingredients. Fill the glass with crushed ice, studding the drink with cherries. Garnish the top of the Pirate's Dream with cherries and decorate the rim of the glass with a slice of orange and a slice of lemon. Place 8 to 10 straws into the drink and serve.

8 to 10 Servings

2	*sprigs of fresh mint*
1	*ounce Jamaican rum*
1	*ounce 151 proof rum*
2	*ounces Puerto Rican rum*
½	*ounce grenadine*
Juice of 1 orange	
Juice of 1 lemon	
2	*dashes Angostura bitters*
Crushed ice	
8 to 10 maraschino cherries	
1	*orange slice*
1	*lemon slice*

You can relax, doc.

This is no bubbling–over build–up to make you believe "The Pirate's Dream" is the finest drink in America. It isn't, and nobody knows that better than I do.

It won't make you want to go out and sink a ship all by yourself and it won't make you feel you could walk a plank and just not give a damn, either.

It's not guaranteed to make a pirate out of a piker and you can lay your last buck on the barrel–head that it won't make a piker out of a pirate. Look at me, I'm charging a pair of "Iron Men" for the thing.

"The Pirate's Dream" is neither glamorous nor gay. I know that, too.

On the other hand, it's colorful in a deadly sort of way, cooling as a sea breeze, and, I think, kind of classy. In short, "The Pirate's Dream" is the high brow of all low brow drinks. That you can jot down.

First of all, it's a giant of a thing, a 28–ounce job with a rum base, which is as it should be because everybody knows even Jean Lafitte and his mob couldn't swing so much as a cutlass without their skinful of rum. Then, it's got ice and grenadine and mint and a dozen or so other fixtures because, hell, it's the specialty of The Old Absinthe House and I've got to pretty it up for you don't I?

On the intangible side, one of them will make every woman you know look like a queen and every man a mouse, or every woman a witch and every man a mate, depending on you. One of them will also make you see bursts of amethysts and rubies and at the right time if you know just how to handle it, but that's all a matter of delicate timing and control and certainly not something for a firsttimer to be trying.

Anyhow, let's leave it at that for now. If you're the adventuresome type, call the waiter and be sure and give him your name and address so I can have the body delivered, if necessary. If you don't feel adventuresome, don't call the waiter. Don't treat yourself to "The Pirate's Dream". You don't have to, you know.

Nobody's twistin' your arm.

Owen Brennan

RAMOS GIN FIZZ

1 Serving

1½	ounces gin
¼	teaspoon orange flower water
⅛	teaspoon vanilla
¼	teaspoon lemon juice
2	teaspoons simple syrup (see Index)
1	egg white
½	cup half and half
¼	cup crushed ice

*C*ombine all of the ingredients in a blender and blend for 15 seconds. Pour into a chilled old-fashioned glass, then serve.

RED ROOSTER

1 Serving

¾	cup ice cubes
1½	ounces vodka
3	ounces cranberry juice
½	ounce orange juice
1	whole ripe strawberry
1	orange slice

*P*lace the ice cubes in a stemmed glass and add the vodka and cranberry juice. Splash the orange juice into the glass, then garnish with a strawberry and slice of orange.

SAZERAC

Pour ½ teaspoon Pernod or Herbsaint into an old-fashioned glass. Tip the glass and swirl the liqueur to coat the inside. Pour off any excess liqueur.

Combine the remaining ingredients in a cocktail shaker. Shake well, then strain the drink into the prepared glass. Garnish with a lemon twist and serve.

1 Serving

½	teaspoon Pernod or Herbsaint
1½	ounces rye whiskey
2	dashes Angostura bitters
4	dashes Peychaud's bitters
Dash of simple syrup (see Index)	
8	ice cubes
A twist of lemon peel for garnish	

CAFÉ BRULÔT

2 Servings

1	whole orange
1	whole lemon
4	whole cloves
2	cinnamon sticks
1	ounce Grand Marnier
1	ounce cognac
½	ounce cherry brandy (optional)
2	teaspoons sugar
2	cups fresh black coffee

With a sharp knife, peel the orange in one continuous piece, leaving the peel attached to the orange at the base. Peel the lemon in one continuous piece, but do not leave it attached. Stud the orange peel with the cloves.

Break the cinnamon sticks in half and place them into a brulôt bowl (see note below). Add the peeled orange and lemon peel to the bowl and pour the Grand Marnier, cognac, and brandy over the fruit. Sprinkle the mixture with the sugar.

Light a heat source (sterno or alcohol burner) under the bowl and heat the contents over medium high heat until slightly bubbling. Insert a long-handled fork into the orange at the joint of the peel, then flame the mixture. Holding the orange over the bowl, pour the ignited alcohol over the orange with the ladle several times lighting the entire peel. Release the orange from the fork; then pour in the coffee and douse the flames. Strain the coffee mixture into brulôt or demi-tasse cups and serve.

Note: If you do not have a brulôt bowl, this festive drink can also be made in a deep silver bowl. Combine the peeled orange, lemon peel, cinnamon, and sugar in the bowl. Heat the liqueurs on the stove top until bubbling, but do not boil. At the table, pour the hot liqueurs into the bowl and flame the mixture, then follow the recipe instructions above.

CAFÉ PIERRE

❧

*P*our the sugar onto a small plate. Rub the rim of an 8-ounce stemmed glass with the lime, then invert the glass into the sugar.

Pour the brandy into the glass and gently warm the glass over a sterno or alcohol burner to flame the brandy and candy the sugar. Add the Kahlua and Galliano, then slowly fill the glass with the coffee. Top with the whipped cream and sprinkle with instant coffee.

1 Serving

3	*teaspoons sugar*
A wedge of lime	
¾	*ounce brandy (Cognac can be substituted.)*
½	*ounce Kahlua*
¼	*ounce Galliano*
¾	*cup fresh black coffee*
¼	*cup whipped cream*
1	*teaspoon instant coffee*

DRINKS 277

BRENNAN'S IRISH COFFEE

1 Serving

1¼	ounces Irish whiskey
2	sugar cubes
¾	cup fresh black coffee
¼	cup whipped cream
1	teaspoon instant coffee

Combine the whiskey and sugar cubes in an 8-ounce stemmed glass or mug. Pour the coffee into the glass and top with whipped cream. Sprinkle with instant coffee and serve.

NUTTY IRISHMAN

1 Serving

¾	cup crushed ice
1½	ounces Irish cream liqueur
¾	ounce Frangelico
¼	cup half and half

Place the crushed ice in an old-fashioned glass. Pour the remaining ingredients over the ice and stir well.

Brennan's Shamrock

❦

Combine the ingredients in a cocktail shaker. Shake well, then pour into chilled glasses.

1 Serving

1½ ounces Irish whiskey
¼ ounce blue curaçao
¼ cup pineapple juice
¾ cup crushed ice

Simple Syrup

❦

Combine the sugar and water in a small saucepan and boil for 5 minutes. Transfer to a glass jar and store in the refrigerator.

Yields 1 cup

1 cup sugar
½ cup water

INDEX

ORDER FORM

❧

$\mathcal{P}$lease send me

_____ copies of *Breakfast at Brennan's and Dinner, Too,* at $27.50 each.

Orleans Parish residents add $2.48 (9% city and state sales tax) $_____

Louisiana state residents add $1.10 (4% state sales tax only) $_____

Postage and handling at $5.00 each $_____

Total $_____

Mail cookbook(s) to:

Name _____ Phone (_____) _____–_____

Address _____

City _____ State _____ Zip _____

Make checks payable to Brennan's Inc.

Charge to (check one):   ☐ VISA   ☐ MasterCard   ☐ American Express   ☐ Discover

☐ Diners Club/Carte Blanche   ☐ JCB

Account Number _____ Valid thru _____

Signature _____

Mail to: BRENNAN'S RESTAURANT
417 Royal Street
New Orleans, Louisiana 70130-2191

Phone Orders: 504-525-9713
or
Fax: 504-525-2302